CW00456005

The essential
handbook to
the world's finest
spa experiences

Image: Pimalai Resort & Spa, Thailand, Page 65

Image: Conrad Maldives Rangali Island, Page 16

Contents

Top Tips

Spa guru, Issy von Simson, Beauty Director at Tatler, offers some personal insight and invaluable advice that every Luxury Spa traveller should know.

So who wants to hear the truth about spas? The hints and tips that you wish someone had told you before you got there: the off-the-menu treatments that you'd be crazy to miss, the therapists that you must request, and crucially, the clothes that you should and should not wear. Here's a little taster:

So, to the SHA Wellness Clinic in Spain. A full on, committed, million-pronged attack on your health and fitness, with spectacular views over the bright lights of the Costa Blanca. You'll be measured and weighed, given the most thorough of medical evaluations, and served small portions of macrobiotic food, but it's all in the name of feeling so so much better. If you have plumped for the starvation menu, just make sure you don't leave the compound or your resolve will be tested by the tempting wafts of tapas from nearby restaurants.

Further south, at the blissful spa at Royal Mansour Marrakesh, the outrageously opulent palace owned by the King of Morocco, you can loll around in the beautiful hammams, work up a sweat in the high-tech gym, have your hair coiffed and nails buffed to a shine. But what you'd be mad to skip is the world's only Chanel beauty room on the top floor. Be sure to book an appointment, this is your chance.

Up in the Himalayas at the utterly serene Ananda there's one thing you mustn't forget to pack: your watch. Manager Mr Khanna dislikes clocks. In fact, you won't find one anywhere and it is amazingly relaxing but if you are the kind of person that needs to know the time, don't leave your Swatch behind. One thing that can safely stay at home though, are your pjs. Ananda provides a crisp pair of kurta pyjamas every morning, which are perfect for yoga.

Over at Parrot Cay & COMO Shambhala Retreat in the ever-sunny Turks and Caicos Islands, those pristine Heidi Klein kaftans can stay in the wardrobe. They have a 24-hour "spa" room service menu so you can order ultra-healthy breakfasts, lunches and suppers - grilled chicken, quinoa with dates and nuts, fruit sorbets - without having to move an inch from your super-smart villa. But if you can tear yourself away, do try a meditation session on the lagoon side of the island. There's a bubbling, "boiling" hole just past Mrs Ong's yoga pavilion that's completely tranquil and hidden.

The best thing about the Lion in the Sun Retreat in Kenya is that no-one seems to know that it exists. A detox? In Africa? What a perfect bolt-on at the end of an indulgent safari. Make sure you ask to see Marga, who runs the spa. She is an energy healer and will come and work her magic (perhaps a spot of reiki) while you are having an algae wrap. Honestly, she has bewitching powers.

So the key, people, is to do your research, to read reviews, to speak to friends, to the concierge at the hotel, to ask questions and get the inside track. It'll make all the difference between a good and a fabulous trip. You heard it here first.

Image: The Banjaran Hotsprings Retreat, Malaysia, Page 53

Asian Roots

Geeta Rao, Contributing Editor, Vogue India, and eminent writer for various luxury and wellness publications, explores Asia's influence in modern day spas.

Tucked away amongst temples and the reclining Buddha is Bangkok's Wat Pho, the origin of traditional Thai massage. Within the complex is an open air school where you can either enrol to become a master or mistress of the world famous Thai massage or simply experience the benefits of it first-hand in its spiritual birthplace.

For those seeking authentic Asian treatments such as lomi lomi massage and tui na in a more opulent setting, there is now a wealth of international luxury spas boasting the finest therapists and exceptional facilities to delight even the most discerning traveller.

At Capella Singapore's Auriga Spa, Baba and Nyonya traditions sit comfortably with Malay Islamic practices. The spa itself bases all its treatments around the waxing and waning of the moon as prescribed by the Chinese lunar calendar. Its Porcelain Moon ritual with peony and plum blossoms reflects the local Peranakan Chinese heritage while the Mandi Safar bath, inspired by an annual bathing ritual prescribed in the Muslim month of Safar, offers you a journey enveloped in attar, buttermilk, and sandalwood and rose oils.

At Ananda in the Himalayas, a renowned favourite with seasoned spa goers, the Ananda Fusion massage combines numerous massage techniques from around the world with dosha balancing oils. Yet it is the strict emphasis on classic Ayurveda and cleansing Panchakarma programmes that Ananda is better known for. New to discover is the more intense shatkriya based on the 6 detoxifications prescribed in hatha yoga.

Spectacular destinations can add a whole new dimension to treatments and few can match the Jiva Grande Spa at Taj Exotica in the Maldives or Malaysia's Banjaran Hotsprings Retreat located in the limestone hills and caves of Ipoh. The Banjaran has geothermal springs, ice baths and a thermal steam cave but it also offers urut, the Malay massage.

The Jiva spa brand continues its exploration of more classic rituals and yoga therapies. Alepa, the ritual anointing of the body that derives from royal India, is their signature treatment. Jiva is now working with the Bihar School of Yoga to develop therapies and practices based on the purest form of classical yoga.

Harnessing thousands of years of Eastern healing wisdom, Ayurveda, yoga and Thai massage have now become ubiquitous offerings in Western spas. Similarly, there is a growing trend for Asian spas to expand their treatment menus with Western influenced, medically focused therapies. Vichy showers, floatation tanks and water jets, Swedish massages and Hungarian mud packs with state-of-the-art facilities are not hard to come by in Asia.

Asia's unequalled culture of the spa is seeped in ancient healing systems and time-honoured rituals. These beliefs are immediately evident in sensitively curated spa treatment menus within Asia and beyond. As spa philosophies evolve and draw upon both local rituals and Western ideologies, an exciting fusion of the traditional with scientific innovation is redefining the concept of the modern day spa.

Spa Cuisine

Dr Lee Nelson, Director of Split Apple Retreat, New Zealand, discusses the scientific importance of food for health.

We've all been brought up believing in "no pain - no gain" and that food's no different. Eating healthily meant denying ourselves the foods we love, replacing them with tiny portions of the dull or unappetising. Amid epidemics of obesity, diabetes and general ill-health, the good news is that food can be both healthy and delicious.

Consider this: The USA's National Cancer Institute attributes more than one third of all cancers to dietary factors. One third! That's an incredible statistic.

Fabulous food can contribute to good health, fight ageing, assist weight loss, combat stress, crank up energy levels and promote longevity, if thoughtfully selected and prepared. This is what the best spa cuisines are all about.

Top spa recipes use low glycemic index (GI) foods, stabilising blood sugar levels and reducing cravings, along with foods known to decrease inflammation, a condition underlying degenerative diseases including cancer, Alzheimer's, heart disease, diabetes, strokes and arthritis.

So what causes inflammation? Well, it's all linked to the same processes that mess with your blood sugar when you don't eat the right food (or too much of the wrong stuff).

A lot has been recently written about low-carb diets. Carbohydrates aren't all bad - fruits and vegetables are rich in good carbs and should be liberally consumed. Carbs from sugar and processed foods, on the other hand, are counterproductive and should be avoided.

Carbohydrates are categorised according to the GI (glycemic index) i.e. how rapidly they get converted to glucose. The higher the GI, the faster your blood sugar peaks and falls after eating, leaving you craving more carbs.

Insulin metabolises glucose. Over time, a resistance to insulin develops and that leads to higher base levels of blood sugar and insulin, increasing the extremes of the sugar/insulin relationship - you get bigger sugar highs and deeper insulin lows.

That's a big enough issue in itself - you will end up feeding your sugar addiction and, as a result, slamming on the extra pounds - but elevated blood sugar and insulin levels are also closely linked to increased inflammation.

Sugar is then converted to fat and fat deposits work like a gland releasing more pro-inflammatory substances, adding fuel to inflammation's fire. Spa food combines the beneficial carbs from a wide variety of fruits and vegetables with fish, seafood, egg whites and free-range poultry as sources of protein.

Nuts and healthy oils such as olive oil are the primary sources of beneficial fats. And deprivation is definitely not on the menu! Medical studies have shown that moderate consumption of red wine (up to 2 glasses per day) has a positive impact on longevity and dark chocolate (minimum of 70% cocoa) helps protect against heart disease.

Nutritionally-balanced spa cuisine reduces inflammation directly and combats weight gain (an indirect source of inflammation) as well as reducing sugar cravings. Best of all, you will come away with ideas that you can readily incorporate into your daily home routine - differences that really will make a difference!

Africa, Indian Ocean & Middle East

Spas in the Middle East combine the ancient traditions and medical philosophies of Arabia with contemporary Western practises to tantalise and rejuvenate the senses. Savour indulgent hammam and rasul rituals using aromatic indigenous ingredients such as frankincense, honey, salts, rose and cinnamon oil, widely believed to have healing effects.

Image: Bab Al Shams Desert Resort & Spa, United Arab Emirates, Page 33

Hilton Luxor Resort & Spa

PO Box 13, New Karnak, Luxor, Egypt

Tel: +2 095 23 999 99 **E-Mail:** reservation.luxor@hilton.com **Web:** www.condenastjohansens.com/hiltonluxor

Hilton Luxor Resort & Spa stands on the east bank of the River Nile, moments away from some of the world's most important historic sites. All guest rooms and suites boast spacious bathrooms and private balconies looking out to beautiful views of landscaped gardens or the River Nile. There are no less than 8 restaurants and bars presenting a variety of cuisines such as flavoursome Asian delicacies at Silk Road restaurant and casual poolside dining at Olive restaurant. Admire the breathtaking views with a cocktail at the Sunset Lounge & Terrace and retreat to Nayara Spa for some well-deserved pampering. A wellness sanctuary with 12 private treatment pavilions, Nayara Spa hosts a blend of ancient Egyptian style treatments with state-of-the-art spa practises. Experience nourishing wraps, amethyst steam baths, traditional massages and the extensive facilities that include a whirl infinity pool, an ice fountain and thermal areas for men and women. After an treatment relax further in the beautiful spa courtyard or savour a herbal tea and healthy fruit drink at the spa's Jannah tea bar.

Key Treatments: • Black Sand Body Scrub and Massage • Soothing Bath with Head Massage • Personalised Massage

Key Products: • Anne Sémonin

Kempinski Hotel Aqaba Red Sea

King Hussein Street, PO Box 1441, 77110 Aqaba, Jordan

Tel: +962 3 209 0888 **E-Mail:** sales.aqaba@kempinski.com **Web:** www.condenastjohansens.com/kempinskiaqaba

A watery wonderland on the rocky Jordanian coastline, Kempinski Hotel Aqaba Red Sea is one of the Golden Triangle's most magical destinations. Boasting breathtaking desert scenery and steeped in historical legend, the resort benefits from fantastic local attractions such as close proximity to the ancient lost city of Petra and the valley of Wadi Rum. Glossy marble floors, panoramic views across the Red Sea and sprawling suites - the Royal Suite comes with a personal chef and use of a private yacht - makes the hotel one of the most luxurious in the Gulf of Aqaba, whilst the 3 restaurants showcase truly mouth-watering fare, from casual dining on the beach-front to simple seafood and haute cuisine. No trip is complete without a visit to Kempinski The Spa, a haven of tranquillity with ocean view treatment rooms and a menu of utterly indulgent therapies. Inspired by nature's healing and restorative powers, treatments aim to repair the body's equilibrium. Be sure to book in for a spot of traditional thalassotherapy powered by purifying Arabic water.

Key Treatments: • Mother of Pearl Body Polish • Swedish Massage Using Aloe Vera, Cucumber & Cooling Stones • Dead Sea Salts Exfoliation

Key Products: • Elemental Herbology

KEMPINSKI HOTEL ISHTAR DEAD SEA

Swaimeh, Dead Sea Road, PO Box 815554, 11180 Dead Sea, Jordan

Tel: +962 5 356 8888 **E-Mail:** reservation.ishtar@kempinski.com **Web:** www.condenastjohansens.com/kempinskideadsea

Located on the banks of the Dead Sea, at the lowest point of Earth, is the imposing Kempinski Hotel Ishtar. Each of the elegantly designed rooms and suites has a private balcony looking out to panoramic views across the Dead Sea and beyond. For the ultimate in secluded indulgence be sure to book an Ishtar Royal Villa with private infinity edge pool and butler service. Soak up the Arabian sun by the stylish palm tree lined sunken pool and visit the hotel's exclusive beach to enjoy floating weightlessly in the therapeutic waters of the Dead Sea. 4 restaurants and bars offer Italian and Thai fusion cuisine as well as modern Arabic fare. Finish a delicious meal with the traditional flavoured water pipe. The Anantara Spa is housed in a stunning glass building with a beautiful Dead Sea indoor pool, hydrotherapy pools and secluded relaxation areas. The largest spa in the Middle East, the 27 spacious treatment rooms offer locally inspired therapies such as Dead Sea Body Wraps as well as signature Anantara treatments in luxurious surroundings.

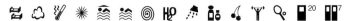

Key Treatments: • Traditional Thai Massage • Dead Sea Mud Wrap • Royal Hammam Ritual

Key Products: • Anantara Signature Blends

MÖVENPICK RESORT & SPA DEAD SEA

Sweimeh, Dead Sea Road, PO Box 815538, Amman 11180, Jordan

Tel: +962 5 356 11 11 **E-Mail:** Resort.deadsea.spa@moevenpick.com **Web:** www.condenastjohansens.com/moevenpick

Mövenpick Resort & Spa Dead Sea stands on the northeastern shore of the Dead Sea. The resort is constructed in the style of a traditional stone village, with a river meandering through its gardens and 9 restaurants and bars surrounding the "village" square. There are also 3 swimming pools, 2 tennis courts and a dedicated children's pool and playground. The 346 rooms and suites feature every modern comfort and showcase handcrafted wood and beautiful fabrics. The Dead Sea is renowned for its therapeutic effects and here, at the lowest point on earth, there is also a Zara Spa offering a higher form of well-being. Enjoy a traditional Eastern hammam, unwind in the mosaic-domed thermariums or savour a refreshing mint-scented tropical rain shower. Experience the benefits of the indoor floatation and kneipp foot massage pools, and take a dip in the hydro-pool or infinity pool. Treatments are held in the privacy of exclusive Royal Therapy suites, with discreet access to the ladies-only fitness suite and relaxation terrace. After your treatments, lie back in a whirlpool and admire the sunset.

Key Treatments: • Natural Dead Sea Salt Scrub • Relaxing Mud Wrap • Shiatsu Massage

Key Products: • Rivage • Thalgo

LION IN THE SUN RETREAT

Marine Park Road, PO Box 1056, 80200 Malindi, Kenya

Tel: +254 725 906044 **E-Mail:** res@liongroup.co.ke **Web:** www.condenastjohansens.com/lioninthesun

Lion in the Sun is an exclusive retreat near Malindi on Kenya's stunning coast. Nestled amidst frangipani, bougainvillea and coconut trees are traditional living units with authentic African interiors. For active guests, there is an intimate state-of-the-art gym with resident instructor and 4 glistening pools filled with salt-water drawn directly from the sea. Just 300 metres away, within the Malindi Marine Park, is the resort's private beach where guests can relax beneath poolside tents while admiring the Indian Ocean. Cuisine at Lion in the Sun is inspired by Italy; memorable dinners are savoured beneath the stars or within the romantic candlelit summer house. One of the highlights of Lion in the Sun is its acclaimed Thalaspa Henri Chenot. The spa offers a range of body and thalassotherapy treatments, combining advanced clinical and physiological techniques with the principles of ancient Chinese medicine to restore the body's natural equilibrium. The exceptional week-long detox package comprises a personalised bio-light diet, massages, hydrotherapy and mud therapy treatments.

Key Treatments: • Massage with Vacuum Cups • Hydrotherapy Using Natural Sea Water • Phyto-mud Therapy

Key Products: • Henri Chenot

CONRAD MALDIVES RANGALI ISLAND

Rangali Island 2034, Republic of Maldives

Tel: +960 668 0629 **E-Mail:** MLEHI.Maldives@conradhotels.com **Web:** www.condenastjohansens.com/conradmaldives

Set against the azure backdrop of the Indian Ocean, Conrad Maldives Rangali Island resort offers complete escapism. Spilling across 2 lush tropical islands and accessed via seaplane, this magical retreat has something for everyone. Steps away from the soft white sand beach, beach villas showcase open air bathrooms that blend seamlessly into the surrounding gardens, whilst elegant water villas with secluded sun decks and plunge pools stand upon stilts in the lapping ocean. For those seeking pure relaxation, the retreat water villas boast private treatment rooms and a deck with Jacuzzi. Luxury suites over the water and on the beach are also available. By day, this paradise is home to some of the world's most incredible diving, and as dusk falls guests can enjoy the blazing sunsets and dine in the spectacular underwater restaurant. The resort has not just one but 2 exceptional spas: the luxurious Spa Retreat marooned in the lagoon with a menu of holistic therapies; and the stunning Over-Water Spa where you can catch a glimpse of the coral reef through glass-floored treatment rooms.

Key Treatments: • Chocolate Truffle Body Wrap • Champagne Sugar Scrub • Signature Facial Using Champagne, Chocolate and Essential Oils

Key Products: • Terraké • Éminence Organic Skin Care • Valmont

HILTON MALDIVES IRU FUSHI RESORT & SPA

PO Box 2036, Noonu Atoll, Republic of Maldives

Tel: +960 656 0591 **E-Mail:** Info.Irufushi@hilton.com **Web:** www.condenastjohansens.com/hiltonmaldives

Sparkling turquoise vistas, heady tropical blooms and the softest white sand beaches make staying at the Hilton Maldives Iru Fushi Resort & Spa a feast for the senses. Set on the exotic island of Noonu Atoll, a pear shaped drop in the Indian Ocean, the resort is a 45-minute seaplane ride from Male and effortlessly blends 5-star hospitality with luxurious accommodation. Guest rooms boast private courtyards and rain showers whilst Water Villas afford sprawling sun decks and glass panelled floors for watching the magical marine life. Meals are best taken alfresco, under the stars at the elegant Flavours restaurant with its aromatic Asian menu or at Islander's Grill which serves simple but flavoursome fare by the beach. Active guests will be spoilt for choice with a range of activities including scuba diving, sailing and swimming in the resort's kaleidoscopic infinity pool. But every guest should make time to indulge at The Spa, a little pocket of peace with 20 generously sized treatment pavilions where traditional Ayurvedic practices have been given a modern twist.

Key Treatments: • Mocha Mud Bodywrap • Exfoliating Scrub with Essential Oils and Sugar • Chocolate Scrub

Key Products: • Thalgo

Shangri-La's Villingili Resort and Spa, Maldives

Villingili Island, Addu Atoll, Maldives

Tel: +960 689 7888 **E-Mail:** slmd@shangri-la.com **Web:** www.condenastjohansens.com/slmd

This is the first luxury Maldives resort south of the equator. Amidst lush vegetation, on spectacular white sandy beaches, this all-villa resort has an exceptional boutique-style atmosphere. Stylish accommodation includes ocean retreats and beach villas with infinity pools, and tropical tree house villas unique to the Maldives. The selection of fine dining choices includes Dr. Ali, which comprises 3 distinctive living rooms representing the cultures of the Indian Ocean, South China Sea and Arabian Gulf. Enjoy a variety of aquatic activities, explore nearby islands by bicycle or savour lunch on a luxury yacht above the equator. CHI, The Spa at Shangri-La is a secluded sanctuary devoted to peace and well-being. Located in a dedicated spa village, spacious treatment villas within private gardens create "spa-within-a-spa" environments. Each features a steam room, changing room and shower. The yoga pavilion overlooks the Indian Ocean. The range of innovative spa treatments covers Asian massages and Indian Ayurvedic treatments as well as locally inspired treatments and wellness programmes.

Key Treatments: • Signature Cowrie Shell Experiences • Ear Candling • Signature Mother of Pearl Polish

Key Products: • CHI, The Spa • Futuresse • Air Spa • Locally Produced Virgin Coconut Oil

Taj Exotica Resort & Spa

PO Box 2117, South Male Atoll, Maldives

Tel: +960 664 22 00 **E-Mail:** exotica.maldives@tajhotels.com **Web:** www.condenastjohansens.com/exoticamaldives

Reached by luxury speedboat, this exclusive resort extends along the length of a picture-perfect private island encircled by the turquoise waters of one of the Maldives' largest lagoons. 64 luxurious palm thatched villas are set amidst the island's verdant tropical vegetation and along stilted over-water walkways radiating out from the island. Each is beautifully appointed in Maldivian style and enjoys captivating views, some have bathtubs overlooking the ocean, others boast private plunge pools. Take a dip in the freshwater infinity pool, enjoy a range of water sports, or take a guided diving excursion to explore the Maldives' colourful underwater world. An authentic Indian spa in the most blissful of settings, Jiva Grande Spa offers an extensive range of treatments and signature experiences. Blending ancient Indian wisdom with contemporary practices, it provides the finest rejuvenating therapies, from aromatic body scrubs and wraps to traditional Ayurvedic therapies. Each of the over-water spa pavilions has a private sundeck and relaxation space from which to gaze out over the lagoon.

Key Treatments: • Signature Facial • Indian Aromatherapy • Ayurveda
Key Products: • Jiva Spa Bespoke Products • Traditional Ayurveda Herbal Oils

DINAROBIN HOTEL GOLF & SPA

Le Morne Peninsula, Mauritius

Tel: +230 401 4900 **E-Mail:** Dinarobin@bchot.com **Web:** www.condenastjohansens.com/dinarobin

Dinarobin Hotel Golf & Spa is located against the dramatic backdrop of Le Morne Mountain on the pristine sandy south coast of Mauritius. All of the resort's Luxury Suites are tastefully decorated in colonial style with traditional thatched roofs, spacious bathrooms and private balconies. The indulgent Club Junior Beach Front Suites boast superior beach-front locations. The resort's 4 restaurants offer guests a culinary journey from Tuscan flavours and French gastronomy with a Mauritian twist to informal beach-side dining. For active guests there are numerous land and water sports to enjoy and for those in need of pampering The Dinarobin Spa by Clarins, nestled amidst lush vegetation, provides a sanctuary of exotic indulgence. Inspired by the Indian practice of Ayurveda, a substantial range of authentic therapies is available to experience within indoor and outdoor treatment cabins. Extensive facilities include hammams, saunas and hydrotherapy pools. After a treatment take a dip in the slate lined spa pool followed by a refreshing tropical cocktail.

Key Treatments: • Ayurvedic Therapies • Extra Firming Facial Using Vitamin D Precursors • Signature Relaxing Massage Using Essential Oils

Key Products: • Clarins

Heritage Le Telfair Golf & Spa Resort

Domaine de Bel Ombre, Mauritius

Tel: +230 601 55 00 **E-Mail:** info@heritageletelfair.mu **Web:** www.condenastjohansens.com/heritageletelfair

Located at the heart of Domaine de Bel Ombre, on a beautiful stretch of pristine white sand beach, stands Heritage Le Telfair comprising 20 villas with 158 rooms and suites amidst lush tropical vegetation. Each is in keeping with French colonial design, inspired by the naturalist Charles Telfair, whilst providing every modern amenity. Ocean suites look out to stunning Indian Ocean views and senior suites include a lounge and dining area adorned with antique furniture. Various dining options include Pan-Asian cuisine, Mediterranean influenced grills at the new C Beach Club and Mauritian cuisine at the exclusive Château de Bel Ombre. Seven Colours Spa - Millesime Collection is a complete wellness destination offering yoga sessions as well as massage and relaxation classes. Its menu of holistic therapies is drawn from the Mauritian culture of caring, allowing guests to find a deep sense of harmony and unwind through tailored treatments. For couples, there are romantic private suites to experience side-by-side treatments in addition to a private relaxation area with outdoor bath.

Key Treatments: • Signature Mauritian Massage With Botanical Oils • Hot Stone Massage • Rhythmical Massage Synchronised to Music

Key Products: • Own Bespoke Locally Sourced Natural Product Range

MARADIVA VILLAS RESORT & SPA

Wolmar, Mauritius

Tel: +230 403 1500 **E-Mail:** reservation@maradiva.com **Web:** www.condenastjohansens.com/maradiva

Against the dramatic backdrop of the Tamarin and Rempart Mountains, where the sands of Tamarin Bay are lapped by iridescent waters, Maradiva Villas Resort offers sheer escapism. The 65 spacious suite villas ($163m^2$-$345m^2$) with private pools, scattered amidst 27 acres of lush vegetation, are decorated in an elegant contemporary style with Indian, African, Mauritian and French Colonial highlights, and offer exotic open air garden showers. Beside a pristine 750m stretch of beach, the tranquil lagoon's clear waters teem with marine life and a variety of water activities are available. A tropical haven for relaxation, Maradiva Spa provides an extensive menu of time honoured Ayurvedic practices and Western healing therapies, each using natural products and oils. Couples will enjoy the romantic candlelit Indian aromatherapy massage followed by a rose petal bath and Champagne on ice. Individual or group yoga sessions take place at the meditation pavilion. As the sun sets, unwind at the alfresco bar, Breakers, before savouring superb Pan-Asian cuisine at Cilantro beneath the stars.

Key Treatments: • Ayurveda • Aromatherapy Massages • Traditional Treatments with Indian Herbs
Key Products: • Subtle Energies • AVP Ayurveda Oils

Sofitel So Mauritius Bel Ombre

Beau Champs, 0 Bel Ombre, Mauritius

Tel: +230 605 58 00 **E-Mail:** H6707-re@sofitel.com **Web:** www.condenastjohansens.com/sofitelsomauritius

Amidst lush vegetation on Mauritius' south coast stands the majestic Sofitel So Mauritius Bel Ombre. All 92 luxury suites and villas boast stylish Asian interiors created from natural materials sympathetic to the jungle location. Each suite and villa has a private garden or plunge pool and most have uninterrupted Indian Ocean views. The signature lounge style restaurant La Plage serves delicious Mauritian cuisine accompanied by striking lagoon views, whilst Le Flamboyant presents an exciting fusion of local flavours with French savoir-faire. Enjoy the complimentary water sports from the nearby white sand beach and visit the tranquil So Spa nestled within verdant gardens for tropical relaxation. The spa houses 6 treatment rooms, 2 wet rooms and a range of facilities including spa pools and hammam. It combines the refinement and skill of the latest in French cosmetology with worldwide ancient traditions to offer an array of massages and indulgent body treatments using natural ingredients including coco, pineapple and hibiscus, and essential oils such as ylang-ylang, sandalwood and vetiver.

Key Treatments: • Energetic Massage • Signature Hibiscus Therapy with Body Scrub, Clay Wrap & Back Massage • Anti-Ageing Acupuncture

Key Products: • Clé Des Champs

ROYAL MANSOUR MARRAKECH

Rue Abou Abbas El Sebti, 40 000 Marrakech, Morocco

Tel: +212 5 29 80 80 80 **E-Mail:** experience@royalmansour.ma **Web:** www.condenastjohansens.com/royalmansour

Set into Marrakech's historic city wall, Royal Mansour is a stunning rendering of a traditional medina. 53 riads, connected by winding alleyways, surround tranquil Andalucían courtyards. Each comprises a spacious living area with bedrooms on the first floor; some have a dining room. Roof terraces with sun beds and private pools provide unrivalled views over the High Atlas Mountains and beyond. No expense has been spared in creating an iconic luxury destination. Exquisite Moroccan furnishings feature throughout, from striking silks and brocades to ornate handcrafted tiles, intricate woodwork and antique furniture. Underground tunnels between the riads enable staff to provide attentive yet unobtrusive service. Within the exotic gardens, a glazed pavilion encircled by a moat houses the impressive spa. Natural Moroccan products, inspired by ancient beauty rituals, release delicate aromas of Arabian rose, sweet almond and orange flower. An authentic hammam at the heart of the spa offers a truly unique experience.

Key Treatments: • Aromatic Massage with Argan Oil • Signature Hammam Massage • Signature Hammam Ritual with Detoxifying Body Mask

Key Products: • Maroc Maroc • Sisley • Dr Hauschka • Chanel

HILTON SEYCHELLES LABRIZ RESORT & SPA

Silhouette Island, PO Box 69, Mahe, Republic of Seychelles

Tel: +248 4293949 **E-Mail:** sezlb.info@hilton.com **Web:** www.condenastjohansens.com/hiltonseychelles

Set on a palm fringed beach on the unspoilt island of Silhouette, a short boat ride away from the main Seychelles island of Mahe, is the magnificent all-villa Hilton Seychelles Labriz Resort & Spa. Each stunning villa accommodation comprises a spacious living area with outdoor rain shower and a private garden overlooking the Indian Ocean or dramatic Mount Dauban. Some of the larger Deluxe Villas and Suites feature beautiful Indian Ocean views and private swimming pools. Guests can choose to dine in one of the resort's 7 elegant restaurants and bars for a variety of delicious fare including local Creole specialities and seafood served alfresco. The Silhouette Spa, surrounded by lush vegetation amongst granite boulders, is a chic haven of relaxation. The treatment menu offers an enticing blend of holistic therapies from around the world using locally sourced island ingredients as well as natural Australian plants and bush flower extracts. Couples can experience treatments together in the luxurious couples' suite followed by a glass of champagne under the tropical skies.

Key Treatments: • Balinese Massage • Earth Stone Massage • Aromatherapy Massage

Key Products: • LI'TYA

RAFFLES PRASLIN, SEYCHELLES

Anse Takamaka, Praslin, Republic of Seychelles

Tel: +248 4 296 000 **E-Mail:** praslin@raffles.com **Web:** www.condenastjohansens.com/rafflespraslin

The new 30-acre, all-villa Raffles Praslin, Seychelles resort is located on the granite island of Praslin, a 15-minute seaplane ride from Mahe. Framed by tropical vegetation, powder white beaches and the Indian Ocean, it comprises 86 villas. Each boasts an open air balcony, outdoor rain shower and private plunge pool. The Royal Panoramic View Villa Suite, located on the highest point of the resort, provides superb ocean views, whilst the 2-bedroomed Raffles Oceanview Villa Suite is ideal for families. Enjoy Creole specialities and international flavours at the resort's selection of bars and restaurants, work out in the state-of-the-art gym, take a dip in the stunning infinity pool and unwind at Raffles Spa. Housed adjacent to the yoga pavilion, the spa is set amidst lush greenery above the turquoise Indian Ocean. The 13 glass-fronted treatment pavilions all offer treatments with spectacular uninterrupted views. The pearl is central to the spa's philosophy of gaining beauty and lustre through a process of rejuvenation and is used throughout the therapies and in beautiful displays within the spa.

Key Treatments: • Shiatsu • Exfoliation Using Therapeutic-Grade Pearl Powder and Soothing Essences • Remineralising Moor Mud Bodywrap

Key Products: • Kerstin Florian

ELLERMAN HOUSE

180 Kloof Road, Bantry Bay, Cape Town 8005, South Africa

Tel: +27 21 430 3200 **E-Mail:** info@ellerman.co.za **Web:** www.condenastjohansens.com/ellerman

Located on the sun-soaked shores of cosmopolitan Cape Town, Ellerman House is a beautiful boutique hotel and host to the Ellerman House Art collection that dates back to 1800 and the newly opened Ellerman Contemporary Gallery. Its 9 exceptionally luxurious guest rooms and 2 suites feature every modern comfort; most have stunning sea views. Food and wine lovers will savour the restaurant's locally inspired African contemporary cuisine paired with award winning wines from the private cellar. Fitness enthusiasts will enjoy the intimate state-of-the-art gym overlooking the Atlantic Ocean and the heated pool set in landscaped gardens. For those seeking pure relaxation there is the Ellerman Spa offering holistic treatments from around the world in a truly sumptuous setting. The varied treatment menu includes traditional Japanese and Swedish massages and homeopathic aromatherapy for complete well-being. After your treatment experience the benefits of the sensation shower or unwind in the infinity pool whilst admiring the views of Cape Town below.

Key Treatments: • La Stone Massage • Sea Salt Body Scrub • Anti-oxidant Facial

Key Products: • Dermalogica • Environ • Lillian Terry International

PEZULA RESORT HOTEL & SPA

Lagoonview Drive, Eastern Head, Knysna, South Africa

Tel: +27 44 302 3333 **E-Mail:** reservations@pezula.com **Web:** www.condenastjohansens.com/pezula

This luxury resort is appropriately named Pezula, an African word meaning "high up with the gods". Surrounded by a beautiful championship golf course, backed by ancient forests of the Southern Cape, Pezula commands sweeping vistas of the Knysna Lagoon and the Indian Ocean. 83 elegantly appointed suites are divided among a series of villas along winding pathways. Contemporary African décor combines warm natural tones and guests will enjoy lazing by the real log fires. The multi award winning spa is a welcoming sanctuary, offering a comprehensive range of the finest treatments and therapies, and uses high-tech equipment alongside indigenous natural products. The state-of-the-art Medi Spa features a comprehensive menu of specialist treatments, carried out by experienced aesthetic medicine practitioners. After your treatments, unwind on a fabulous heated water bed in the relaxation room, a unique offering in Africa.

Key Treatments: • Phumla Signature African Massage • Pezula Colour Balancing Candle Massage • Matombo Hot Stone Experience

Key Products: • RegimA • Dermalogica • Thalgo

SABI SABI PRIVATE GAME RESERVE

Sabi Sands Reserve, Mpumalanga, South Africa

Tel: +27 11 447 7172 **E-Mail:** res@sabisabi.com **Web:** www.condenastjohansens.com/sabisabi

Sabi Sabi Private Game Reserve is set amongst 65,000 unspoiled hectares of South African wilderness in the famous Sabi Sands Reserve, part of Kruger National Park. A truly once-in-a-lifetime experience, guests can watch over 200 species of spectacular wildlife including "the big 5" roaming at close quarters. Accommodation at Sabi Sabi consists of 4 separate luxurious Safari Lodges: Selati Camp; Bush Lodge; Little Bush Camp; and Earth Lodge with the distinct themes of Yesterday, Today and Tomorrow reflected in each Lodge's stylish décor. At Selati Camp 8 opulent suites embrace a colonial "Out of Africa" theme. Bush Lodge and Little Bush Camp feature contemporary African décor and the stunning Earth Lodge is a sanctuary of environmentally friendly design. The Amani Spa at Earth and Bush Lodges offer authentic African holistic body, skin and beauty rituals in an exclusive haven of 4 African inspired treatment cabins. After an indulgent treatment relax in the beautiful Zen meditation garden or take a dip in Earth Lodge's plunge pool under the stunning African stars.

Key Treatments: • African Massage with Rungu Baton • Slimming and Detoxifying Mud Bodywrap • Signature Holistic Body Ritual

Key Products: • Babor • Matsimela Home Spa

Taj Cape Town

Wale Street, Cape Town, South Africa 8001

Tel: +27 21 819 2000 **E-Mail:** res.capetown@tajhotels.com **Web:** www.condenastjohansens.com/tajcapetown

Taj Cape Town is located in Cape Town's vibrant centre, at the entrance to the pedestrian precinct, St George's Mall. Housed within the former South African Reserve Bank and Temple Chambers building, the hotel's style reflects the heritage of the region offset by the finest contemporary amenities. The 177 beautifully decorated rooms and suites are tranquil retreats with views of Cape Town or Table Mountain. Exceptional dining options include The Bombay Brasserie's exceptional Indian cuisine, casual all-day dining restaurant Mint and chic champagne and oyster bar. For pure relaxation there are Jiva Grande Spa's holistic treatments and therapies. The spa's philosophy is rooted in India's ancient healing practices and a profound understanding of the relationship between mind, body and spirit. The extensive menu includes signature and beauty treatments, Indian therapies, scrubs and wraps alongside Cape Fynbos, an African inspired signature experience with soothing Cape Fynbos blend. Afterwards, enjoy the Jacuzzi or indoor heated pool and benefits of the authentic hammam.

Key Treatments: • Detoxifying Exfoliation Ritual • Indian Aromatherapy • Deep Tissue Massage

Key Products: • Jiva Spa Bespoke Products

THANDA PRIVATE GAME RESERVE

D242, Off N2 Between Hluhluwe and Mkuze Hluhluwe, South Africa

Tel: +27 35 573 1899 **E-Mail:** reservations@thanda.co.za **Web:** www.condenastjohansens.com/thanda

Set in the heart of the untamed bush in northern Zululand, Thanda is home to an astonishing variety of wildlife. Thanda means "love" in Zulu, and there can be no more romantic safari destination; in fact, the private game reserve was voted the World's Leading Luxury Lodge at the 2010 World Travel Awards. Stay in one of the 9 beautifully decorated luxury bush villas overlooking the game reserve or enjoy an even more authentic experience at the safari style tented camp. Rise early to join Thanda's knowledgeable guides on a game drive in search of "the big 5" and be sure to take your camera and plenty of film. Spend the afternoon relaxing in your private infinity pool or visit Thanda's unique safari-spa and indulge in a wonderfully aromatic African inspired treatment. In the evening, savour outstanding cuisine beside the campfire and under a canopy of stars. Thanda is a once-in-a-lifetime experience and one that you will want to return to again and again.

Key Treatments: • Sensory Body and Hot Stone Massage • Exfoliating Body Scrub and Invigorating Massage • Hydromassage Bath

Key Products: • Africology

THE CHEDI, MUSCAT

PO Box 946, Al Khuwair, Postcode 133, Muscat, Sultanate of Oman

Tel: +968 24 52 4000 **E-Mail:** chedimuscat@ghmhotels.com **Web:** www.condenastjohansens.com/chedimuscat

Situated on a prime beach-front location overlooking the Gulf of Oman and Hajar mountains, The Chedi, Muscat comprises 158 rooms and suites. Tastefully furnished with an understated elegance, the resort wonderfully fuses Omani architecture with Asian Zen style design. Dining options include a choice of 6 restaurants with indoor and outdoor areas serving Arabic, Asian, Indian, Mediterranean, Japanese-Malay cuisine and seafood. Activities nearby include hiking, game fishing, snorkelling and diving whilst on-site there are 3 swimming pools - 2 adults-only and 1 for families - as well as a 37-metre private beach, sauna, steam room, 2 tennis courts and a brand new 400m^2 health club with Technogym equipment, a Pilates corner and a kinesis wall. For luxurious pampering there is The Spa at The Chedi, Muscat, the largest spa in Muscat with 13 fully self contained spa suites featuring private changing facilities. The Spa specialises in Balinese rituals and uses only organic products.

Key Treatments: • Frangipani and Orange Blossom Himalayan Bath • Abhyanga Massage • Detoxifying Himalayan Crystal Body Polish

Key Products: • ila • VOYA • REN

Bab Al Shams Desert Resort & Spa

PO Box 8168, Dubai, United Arab Emirates

Tel: +971 4 8096100 **E-Mail:** info@meydanhotels.com **Web:** www.condenastjohansens.com/babalshams

Bab Al Shams, meaning "gateway to the sun" in Arabic, is a spectacular sand fortress inspired resort located in the middle of the desert yet only 30 minutes from Dubai city centre. All rooms and suites are decorated with delightful Arabic ornaments, wall hangings and traditional rugs, and feature spacious bathrooms with huge sunken baths. Most junior suites offer uninterrupted desert views, whilst Deluxe and Royal Suites boast private balconies and patios. Enjoy the wealth of world-class dining options, which includes Al Hadheerah Desert Restaurant's delicious traditional Arabic fare served beside a fire pit surrounded by rolling sand dunes. The Satori Spa at Bab Al Shams provides restorative treatments in a sanctuary of Middle Eastern comfort. Treatments include alternative therapies such as reflexology and indulgent spa rituals such as the Satori Extravagance. For a truly unique experience try the monthly sunset yoga session in the desert hosted by the resident Yogi Master. Or for something less taxing, savour a sunset cocktail at the rooftop bar beneath the canopy of the Arabian sky.

Key Treatments: • Signature Massage Using Hawaiian and Balinese Techniques • De-stressing Facial with Massage • Detoxifying Body Wrap

Key Products: • Aromatherapy Associates

FUJAIRAH ROTANA RESORT & SPA

PO Box 1856, Al Aqah Beach, Fujairah, United Arab Emirates

Tel: +971 9 244 9888 **E-Mail:** fujairah.resort@rotana.com **Web:** www.condenastjohansens.com/fujairahrotana

In a magnificent setting, sheltered by the imposing Hajar mountains and overlooking white sand beaches and the Indian Ocean, Fujairah Rotana Resort & Spa is an oasis of exotic gardens, shimmering pools and cascading waterfalls. The 250 rooms and suites blend local architectural features with colonial style and all boast a private balcony or terrace from which to savour the ocean views. In the heat of the day, stroll along the beach, take a dip in the beautiful pool or order a cocktail at the sunken Tropicana pool bar. In the evening, dine at the beachside restaurant Waves or sample Mozaique's international cuisine. Zen the spa at Rotana is a stylish, tranquil retreat offering an extensive menu of holistic Asian therapies. Exclusive 3, 4 and 5 day packages range from relaxation to complete detox programmes, and the spa team will advise on suitable treatments for individuals' needs. For sheer indulgence, experience the Serenity suite with hydrotherapy jet bath and private relaxation area or enjoy an open air massage in a beachside cabana.

Key Treatments: • Personalised Facial • Signature Massage With Essential Oils • Enriching Vitamin E Body Cocoon

Key Products: • Aromatherapy Associates

SHANGRI-LA HOTEL, QARYAT AL BERI, ABU DHABI

Between the Bridges, PO Box 128881, Abu Dhabi, United Arab Emirates

Tel: +971 2509 8888 **E-Mail:** slad@shangri-la.com **Web:** www.condenastjohansens.com/shangrilaabudhabi

Shangri-La Hotel, Qaryat Al Beri, Abu Dhabi is located on a 1 kilometre stretch of beautiful palm-fringed private beach between the bridges that separate Abu Dhabi Island from the mainland. All 214 rooms and suites boast striking modern Arabic décor, each with a spacious balcony offering stunning sea and mosque views. A variety of delectable dining options such as Vietnamese, Cantonese, French, Mediterranean seafood and international cuisine is available. CHI, The Spa at Shangri-La houses a number of facilities including a traditional hammam, peaceful rooftop lap pool, Jacuzzi, fully equipped fitness room and sauna and steam room. The treatment menu features traditional Arabic therapies such as the Arabian Date Ritual and Rose and Honey Body Wrap, Asian wellness massages inspired by ancient Asian healing philosophies and CHI's signature therapies based on the ancient Five Elements Theory in which metal, water, wood, fire and earth are in balance to harmonise with the positive yang and the negative yin energy in the body.

Key Treatments: • Healing Hot Stone Massage • Hammam • Nourishing Envelopment Using Dates, Coconut Milk, Almond and Vanilla

Key Products: • Wild Earth • Futuresse • CHI Bespoke Product Range

Americas, Atlantic & Caribbean

White sand beaches, a tropical climate and a relaxed culture, the Caribbean islands have been a long-time favourite retreat for those in need of rejuvenation. Enjoy alfresco treatments using local ingredients such as green coffee and tropical fruits, and further south experience indulgent Mayan massage rituals and traditional Central American temazcal "sweat lodges".

Image: CuisinArt Golf Resort & Spa, Anguilla, Page 37

CUISINART GOLF RESORT & SPA

PO Box 2000, Rendezvous Bay, Anguilla

Tel: +1 264 498 2000 **E-Mail:** reservations@cuisinart.ai **Web:** www.condenastjohansens.com/cuisinartresort

Nestled in the crescent curve of Rendezvous Bay, CuisinArt Golf Resort & Spa is a sophisticated beach-front resort celebrating the ultimate Caribbean escape. With a choice of 99 luxurious suites and villas, guests are enticed by the magnificent beach, world class spa, acclaimed fine dining restaurants, culinary activities including cooking classes and wine tastings, and the thrilling challenge of the stunning 18 Hole Greg Norman championship course. The award winning Venus Spa is a distinctive retreat with 16 treatment rooms. Its diverse menu includes indulgent Venus Spa Journeys and Rituals as well as the Fresh Escapes therapies, which use ingredients sourced daily from CuisinArt's unique Hydroponic Farm. The Caribbean inspired treatments include the warmed shell massage and the aromatic Anguillan coconut pineapple scrub. The healing waters pool with mineral enriched salt water, is the first aqua therapy pool of its kind in the Caribbean. It features built-in loungers and soothing hydrotherapy jets and is used for signature treatments such as the unique Aqua Massage.

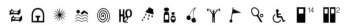

Key Treatments: • Anguillan Coconut Pineapple Scrub • Hydroponic Cucumber and Aloe Wrap • Aqua Massage

Key Products: • Repêchage • ê Shave • Rusk

Spa Unique Garden

Estrada Laramara 3500, Mairiporã, São Paulo 07600-970, Brazil

Tel: +55 11 4486 8700 **E-Mail:** uniquegarden@uniquegarden.com.br **Web:** www.condenastjohansens.com/uniquegarden

Spa Unique Garden adopts a holistic approach to the rejuvenation of body and soul. An oasis of well-being and relaxation it is set within extensive fragrant gardens and woodland filled with exotic plants and birds. The 26 guest apartments range from a welcoming Brazilian farmhouse style to strikingly modern. The resort's 3 restaurants include the wonderful Chez Victor, which is decorated in rich hues lit by votive candles and serves beautifully presented Mediterranean inspired dishes. The spa promotes complete healing and restoration with a menu of over 80 therapies and beauty treatments influenced by the Brazilian, Indian, Chinese, Japanese, European, North American and Mayan cultures. As well as the 21 individually designed private treatment rooms, there are also 5 cabanas in the resort's beautiful grounds dedicated to special therapies such as vinotherapy and Ayurveda. Guided yoga classes take place in the outdoor pavilion and there is a state-of-the-art Pilates studio. All-inclusive 3, 5 and 7 night packages cater for guests' specific needs.

Key Treatments: • Gharshana Massage • 6-Hand Massage • Brazilian Herb Poultice Massage

Key Products: • Germaine de Capuccini • Vyveda • Samya • Bvlgari

Tabacón Grand Spa Thermal Resort

La Fortuna de San Carlos, Arenal, Alajuela, Costa Rica

Tel: +506 2519 1999 **E-Mail:** sales@tabacon.com **Web:** www.condenastjohansens.com/tabacon

Situated in Costa Rica's northern region at the foot of the Arenal Volcano is this carbon-neutral resort offering adventure and relaxation in a rich rainforest setting. The 114 traditionally styled guest rooms feature locally crafted furniture and private decks. The Ave del Paraiso Restaurant is located in the lush gardens and provides buffet style dining as well as dedicated spa cuisine. A natural thermal river flows through the grounds, cascading down picturesque waterfalls and forming 12 hot spring pools and lagoons. The Grand Spa is reached via a series of winding stone pathways and arched bridges, and incorporates the mineral springs into its unique open air environment and various hydrotherapy experiences. Treatments are enjoyed in open air garden bungalows, each with a private Jacuzzi, and guided outdoor yoga sessions and ancient style temazcal (sweat lodges) are available. In addition, the Lifestyle & Wellness Program, which includes Ayurvedic food, advice from a nutritionist, time with a personal trainer and spa treatments using natural ingredients, is not to be missed!

Key Treatments: • Watsu • Volcanic Mud Wraps • Volcanic Hot Stone Massage

Key Products: • Germaine de Capuccini

LaSource

Pink Gin Beach, St George's, Grenada

Tel: +1 473 444 2556 **E-Mail:** reservations@theAmazingHoliday.com **Web:** www.condenastjohansens.com/lasource

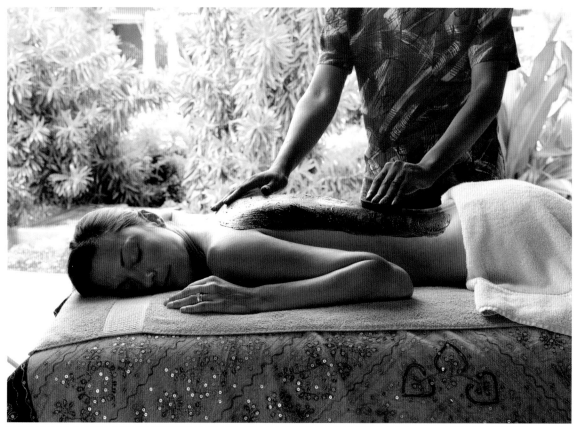

LaSource is found on Grenada's southern tip, on the idyllic Pink Gin Beach. Surrounded on 3 sides by the sea and set amidst tropical gardens, it is a true haven for relaxation and exceptional all-inclusive destination. The 100 colonial style rooms evoke the island's history with striking mahogany furniture, wooden shutters and marble flooring. They also feature private balconies and terraces. A deli and 3 different restaurants, serving various contemporary fusion dishes and traditional specialities, keep guests' palates satisfied. Cuisine LaSource is healthy and nutritious, lighter in calories yet full of flavour. Active guests can enjoy golf, tennis, kayaking and biking, and 3 free scuba diving sessions per stay. Complimentary classes include yoga, t'ai chi and meditation. The Moroccan themed Oasis Spa issues guests with personalised treatment programmes, and a 50-minute treatment each day free of charge. Additional therapies can be booked from the extensive menu for an extra cost; try the spicy Grenadian body scrub or green coffee body wrap for a unique indigenous experience.

Key Treatments: • Thai Massage • Anti-Ageing Caviar Facial • Acupuncture

Key Products: • Pevonia

EL CHANTE SPA HOTEL

Rivera del Lago 170-1, El Chante, Jocotepec, Jalisco 45825, Mexico

Tel: +52 387 763 26 08 **E-Mail:** reserve@elchantespa.com **Web:** www.condenastjohansens.com/elchantespa

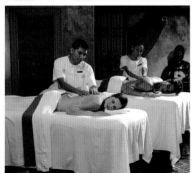

Taking its name from the word "chantli", meaning home, the world class El Chante Spa Hotel aims to harmonise each guest's mind, body and soul through the implementation of ancient and holistic therapies. Set against the Sierra Madre mountains, beside the peaceful Lake Chapala, it provides sheer escapism. Guest rooms are spacious and well-equipped, decorated with vibrant Mexican artwork; most have balconies with lake views. Also facing the lake, Tokal restaurant serves Signature Cuisine which can be enjoyed alfresco or under a large pergola. The spa's treatments are influenced by rituals and cultures from around the world, with treatment spaces styled according to the origins of a particular treatment. Spa programmes combine complementary therapies to promote complete well-being. The Beauty Salon offers the finishing touches. After your treatments relax on a double lounge bed or woven hammock beside the pool and enjoy a cocktail from the poolside bar. Later, talk a stroll through the pretty gardens or experience the soothing immersion bath or steam igloo.

Key Treatments: • Absolute Hydration Facial • Abhyanga 4 Hand Massage • Aromatic Fruit Body Wrap

Key Products: • Germaine de Capuccini • Natura Bisse • Natural Benefits • Essences

HOTELITO DESCONOCIDO SANCTUARY RESERVE & SPA

Playon de Mismaloya S/N, Municipio de Tomatlán, La Cruz de Loreto, Jalisco 48460, Mexico

Tel: +52 33 3611 1255 **E-Mail:** ventas@hotelito.com **Web:** www.condenastjohansens.com/hotelito

Hotelito Desconocido meaning "unknown little hotel" in Spanish, is an ecological retreat in the heart of Costalegre, a 140 mile stretch of coastline featuring virgin sandy beaches, lagoons, rivers and the Sierra Madre. Designed to replicate traditional fishing villages, it epitomises off-the-beaten-track escapism. 27 thatched "palafito" lagoon bungalows are reached by rowing boat; 3 extensive 3-bedroom "ecovillages" are set on the beach. Swim in the beach-side salt-water pool, take a fishing trip to catch supper and savour the open air restaurant's fine regional cuisine. Be sure to visit the biocentre, home to giant marine turtles and over 180 species of protected birds. The holistic spa offers customised programmes with entirely natural, chemical-free products. Its large thalassotherapy area comprises hydrotherapy pools, jets and experience showers; the benefits of which are complemented by algae, mud and salt treatments. Signature therapies draw on ancient practices from Mexico, the Far East and Mediterranean. Spa Rituals, from 5 to 21 days, aid complete relaxation and rejuvenation.

Key Treatments: • Purifying Rose Body Polish • Chocolate Ritual Exfoliation, Body Massage and Facial • Mayan Thai Fusion Massage

Key Products: • Locally Sourced Natural Ingredients

Parrot Cay & COMO Shambhala Retreat

PO Box 164, Providenciales, Turks & Caicos Islands

Tel: +1 649 946 7788 **E-Mail:** res@parrotcay.como.bz **Web:** www.condenastjohansens.com/parrotcay

Parrot Cay resort occupies the northern Caribbean's pre-eminent private 1,000 acre island. Accommodation is modern colonial in style; whitewashed walls, teak furniture and four poster beds swathed in white linen and drapes create inviting and cooling sanctuaries. Verandas with open air daybeds are ideal for unwinding with a holiday read. The holistic COMO Shambhala Retreat at Parrot Cay provides state-of-the-art facilities overlooking the wetlands and offers an extensive Ayurvedic Programme with resident doctor. It pioneered COMO Shambhala spa cuisine and runs Retreat Weeks with the world's best yoga teachers, as well as guided Pilates and personal training sessions. 3, 5 and 7 night Wellness Programmes, such as Ayurvedic and Stress Management, comprise therapies chosen for a specific purpose.

Key Treatments: • Dead Sea Mud Therapy • Ayurvedic Shamana Therapies • Signature Ritual with Massage, Herbal Bolus and Holistic Facial

Key Products: • COMO Shambhala Signature Blends • COMO Shambhala PURIFY Skincare Range • Guinot • Dr Hauschka

Asia, Australasia & Pacific

The vast and time-honoured Asian knowledge of healing coupled with a holistic and spiritual approach to health and well-being makes it the continent with arguably the richest spa culture on earth. Experience traditional Ayurvedic therapies, authentic massages, reflexology, reiki, yoga and meditation, all practised since ancient times.

Image: Evason Ana Mandara - Nha Trang, Vietnam, Page 68

PINCTADA CABLE BEACH RESORT & SPA

10 Murray Road, Cable Beach, Broome 6725, Australia

Tel: +61 8 9193 8388 **E-Mail:** stay@pinctada.com.au **Web:** www.condenastjohansens.com/pinctadacablebeach

The newly opened Pinctada Cable Beach Resort & Spa is a multi award winning resort located a short walk from beautiful Cable Beach in Broome, Western Australia. The 72 graciously sized rooms and suites are luxuriously appointed; some feature private gardens inspired by the local flora of the Kimberley, while the Shinju Pool View Studios boast private balconies overlooking the Maxima Pool. Choose to dine at Selene Brasserie for exceptional cuisine infused with a hint of the Kimberley and influenced by the Middle East, North Africa and Europe, or enjoy alfresco dining at Brizo Pool Bar & Café. The serene Pinctada Spa is amongst the world's best and offers the perfect oasis to nurture and revive based on traditional Australian and ancient Aboriginal healing traditions. The extensive treatments use LI'TYA Spa Care from the Aboriginal Dreamtime, a native Australian botanical product range created from the wisdom of 40,000 years of indigenous plant knowledge. After a revitalising treatment unwind with a glass of champagne at the Nyx cocktail lounge.

Key Treatments: • Anti-Ageing Cocoon • Body Massage Using Aboriginal Techniques • Exfoliation With Desert Salts & Aromatic Oils

Key Products: • LI'TYA Spa Care from the Aboriginal Dreamtime

THE RICHARDSON HOTEL & SPA

32 Richardson Street, Perth, Western Australia 6005, Australia

Tel: +618 9217 8888 **E-Mail:** reservations@therichardson.com.au. **Web:** www.condenastjohansens.com/therichardson

The Richardson Hotel & Spa's curved triangular design forms a striking landmark in leafy West Perth. Located between the Central Business District and the stylish shopping district of Subiaco, this sophisticated yet understated boutique hotel is ideal for business and leisure travellers alike. The 74 spacious guest rooms and suites have been created with the modern traveller in mind, from the stylish décor and rich furnishings to high-tech amenities and pillow menu. Most rooms feature private balconies and city skyline or Kings Park views. The award winning restaurant Opus is one of Perth's hottest dining spots, serving fresh inventive cuisine. The chic urban spa offers the only ESPA treatments in Australia; from advanced facials and indulgent wraps to a range of treatments specifically for male guests, each experience has been developed exclusively for The Richardson drawing from various spa cultures around the world. Between treatments, guests can take a leisurely swim in the heated indoor pool or relax with a fresh juice or herbal tea in the beautiful poolside garden.

Key Treatments: • Holistic Back, Face and Scalp Massage With Hot Stones • Detoxifying Wrap • Age Defying Facial

Key Products: • ESPA

HILTON BORA BORA NUI RESORT & SPA

BP 502 Vaitape, Bora Bora, French Polynesia 98730

Tel: +689 60 33 00 **E-Mail:** info@hilton-borabora.pf **Web:** www.condenastjohansens.com/hiltonborabora

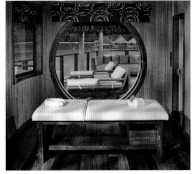

Reached by luxury speedboat, the tropical resort of Hilton Bora Bora Nui Resort & Spa is nestled beside a picture-perfect lagoon on the French Polynesian island of Bora Bora. The 122 over-water villas are furnished in traditional Polynesian style from natural woods and marbles, and feature beautiful exotic artefacts and precious wall hangings. All villas boast private waterside balconies backing directly onto the majestic turquoise waters of the South Pacific and glass floor viewing panels to admire the fascinating marine life. Guests can savour world class Polynesian and Mediterranean flavours at Iriatai restaurant or freshly prepared seafood at Tamure Beach Fare Grill. Perched high on a hilltop surrounded by luscious vegetation, Hina Spa is a haven of natural tranquillity with uninterrupted views of the brilliant blue lagoon below. Given the exceptional location, it is fitting to indulge in the Million Dollar View Experience, which includes an open air body polish and couple's massage using locally sourced, all-natural products.

Key Treatments: • Hot Stone and Cool Shell Massage • Healing and Regenerative Aftersun Care Massage • Signature Foot Bath and Body Polish

Key Products: • NaCr Skin Care and Spa Product Range by Robert Wan Tahiti • Signature Hina Spa Product Range

ANANDA IN THE HIMALAYAS

The Palace Estate, Narendra Nagar, Tehri-Garhwal, Uttaranchal, India

Tel: +91 1378 227500 **E-Mail:** reservation@anandaspa.com **Web:** www.condenastjohansens.com/anandaspa

This multi award winning destination spa is set in the foothills of The Himalayas overlooking the peaceful river Ganga. Its 70 rooms and 5 suites feature balconies and terraces with views of the valley or Maharaja's Palace, and two 2-bedroom villas and one 1-bedroom villa offer private pools and butler service. Ananda provides a holistic journey using traditional Ayurveda, Yoga and Vedanta regimes alongside international wellness techniques. A dedicated team of nutritionists, physicians and therapists guide guests towards a better lifestyle with personalised programmes designed to meet individual needs and health goals. The signature restaurant serves a seasonal menu based on the key principles of Ayurveda and gourmet dining is savoured on the Tree Top Deck. The expansive spa has a beautiful outdoor lap pool, high-tech 16 station life-cycle gym, 24 treatment rooms designed for Ayurveda, Oriental and European therapies and over 80 body and beauty therapies. Special workshops and sessions with visiting Masters as well as a daily schedule of classes and cultural activities are available.

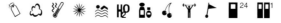

Key Treatments: • Abhyanga • Shirodhara • Tibetan Ku Nye Massage

Key Products: • Own Bespoke Ananda Range • ila

THE LEELA KEMPINSKI GURGAON

Ambience Island, National Highway 8, Gurgaon 122 002, Delhi NCR, India

Tel: +91 124 477 1234 **E-Mail:** reservations.gurgaon-delhi@theleela.com **Web:** www.condenastjohansens.com/leelagurgaon

The Leela Kempinski Gurgaon is conveniently located in New Delhi's NCR region, just a short journey from the capital. Its 322 spacious rooms and suites and 90 serviced apartments are sleek and stylish, and the dining and entertainment options include a range of worldwide cuisines, from international dishes at Spectra to exotic Indian flavours at Diya. The hotel's numerous facilities further include a fully equipped fitness centre and outdoor pool set amidst verdant gardens. Spa Lavanya (lavanya means "beauty and grace" in Sanskrit) is a tranquil and expansive retreat featuring Ayurvedic consultation rooms, personal steam rooms, treatment rooms and spa suites. Each of the treatment rooms has a full bathing area and most overlook the green belt of Gurgaon-Rajokri Greens. The menu covers a range of massages, therapies and specialised treatments. Traditional Indian Ayurvedic therapies are experienced in the wonderfully exotic dedicated Ayurvedic treatment room. After indulgent treatments, lie back on the award winning Alpha lounger and feel any remaining tension melt away.

Key Treatments: • Anti-Ageing Caviar Facial • Hot Stone Therapy • Thalassotherapy

Key Products: • Pevonia

Park Hyatt Goa Resort and Spa

Arossim Beach, Cansaulim, South Goa 403 712, India

Tel: +91 832 272 1234 **E-Mail:** india.reservations@hyatt.com **Web:** www.condenastjohansens.com/parkhyattgoa

Park Hyatt Goa Resort and Spa is set within 45 acres of tropical beach-front gardens in idyllic South Goa. Each contemporary guest room features a balcony or veranda with views of the Arabian Sea or sparkling lagoon. 5 restaurants and 2 bars offer an enticing range of culinary experiences, from the signature fine dining Goan restaurant Casa Sarita to the Palms beach-side grill. The extensive range of activities includes beach volleyball, lawn tennis, archery and water sports, while for children and the young at heart the resort features India's largest swimming pool, complete with water slides. Sereno Spa is a complete wellness destination holding daily yoga and meditation sessions. The spa menu of unique holistic therapies is drawn from the Ayurvedic and Yogic traditions as well as incorporating thalassotherapy, aromatherapy and energy healing. Special packages include the 3 day Skin and Beauty and 5 day Detoxification Programmes, while Ayurvedic Touch Therapies are based on the individual's natural body-mind constitution, customised with specific herbal essences.

Key Treatments: • Ayurvedic Rejuvenating Massage • Pitta Abhyanga • Traditional Marma Facial

Key Products: • Vedaya • Kottakkal Arya Vaidya Sala • THAL'ION • comfort zone

KOMANEKA AT RASA SAYANG

Jalan Monkey Forest, Ubud, Gianyar 80571, Bali, Indonesia

Tel: +62 361 976090 **E-Mail:** sales@komaneka.com **Web:** www.condenastjohansens.com/komaneka

Situated in Ubud, in the spiritual heart of Bali, is Komaneka at Rasa Sayang, a beautiful boutique hotel surrounded by lush vegetation. Each of the 30 spacious deluxe rooms and 2 rooftop garden villas is authentically furnished in Balinese style with polished wood and local exotic silks; some boast a private balcony with views of tropical gardens. Sample traditional Indonesian flavours at the property's restaurant and enjoy daily afternoon tea with local pastries served alfresco. Spend days soaking up the tropical sunshine by the tree lined infinity pool or learn the art of Balinese cuisine by attending a cookery class. Komaneka Akar Wangi Spa offers a host of Balinese inspired therapies in spacious Indonesian styled treatment rooms. All of the 6 treatment rooms overlook the tropical jungle with therapies accompanied by the soothing sound of running water and fragrant aroma of herbs and spices to further relax the mind and body. Komaneka Spa uses an exclusively developed product range that utilises locally sourced natural ingredients.

Key Treatments: • Traditional Full Body Massage and Moisturising Treatment • Traditional Balinese Boreh • Balinese Massage

Key Products: • Bespoke Komaneka Akar Wangi Spa Product Range

PURI MAS BOUTIQUE RESORTS & SPA

Jl. Raya, Mangsit Beach, Senggigi, Lombok NTB, Indonesia

Tel: +62 370 693831 **E-Mail:** info@purimas-lombok.com **Web:** www.condenastjohansens.com/purimas

Puri Mas Boutique Resorts & Spa are situated close to Senggigi and the renowned Senggigi Beach. Between 2 resorts, barely minutes apart, are 36 private pool villas, suites and rooms designed to reflect the unique Indonesian style and culture. Guests are greeted by friendly service, peace and tranquillity. The Ballroom Restaurant at the Beach Resort offers romantic dining beside the ocean, while Puri Mas Spa Resort serves authentic Indonesian flavours on a floating Javanese pavilion. Staff can organise adventure tours to Rinjani Mountain, dive packages to Gili Trawangan, PADI courses, snorkelling trips and much more. At Puri Mas Spa Resort, amidst tropical vegetation and fragrant flowers, beneath gently swaying palms, is the beautiful spa. Enjoy a range of well-being activities, yoga sessions and packages featuring massages and body treatments inspired by ancient local practices using traditional indigenous herbs, spices and oils. For complete relaxation, the signature Full Day experience includes a soothing flower or milk and vanilla bath. Later, take a swim in the designer pool or relax in the pavilion.

Key Treatments: • Age-Defying Facial • Warm Oil Masage and Herbal Compress • Signature Foot Spa Ritual With Massage

Key Products: • Pevonia

THE BANJARAN HOTSPRINGS RETREAT

No 1, Persiaran Lagun Sunway 3, 31150 Ipoh, Perak, Malaysia

Tel: +60 5 210 7777 **E-Mail:** info.kl@thebanjaran.com **Web:** www.condenastjohansens.com/thebanjaran

Surrounded by verdant jungle, towering limestone cliffs, thermal steam caves, geothermal hot springs, dipping pools and waterfalls, The Banjaran Hotsprings Retreat is a unique natural spa. Focusing on healthy living, the retreat's all-inclusive rates include accommodation, spa cuisine, fitness classes, a wellness consultation and treatments for a minimum 2 night stay. Each luxury villa features a plunge pool and open courtyard living room, outdoor Jacuzzi and rainshower, and a personal butler service. Take a leisurely swim in the free-form pool, savour the therapeutic benefits of the reflexology path and find deep relaxation in the meditation cave. The Banjaran Spa & Wellness Centre offers a wide range of therapies with holistic treatments inspired by indigenous Malay, Chinese and Indian cultures. The extensive menu includes Traditional Chinese Medicine, Ayurvedic therapies, Malay healing rituals and contemporary spa treatments using natural ingredients. For an authentic indigenous experience, try the traditional Malay Ramuan Spa Journey.

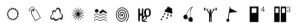

Key Treatments: • Signature Massage • Rejuvenating and Relaxing Facial and Body Treatment • 24 Carat Gold Facial

Key Products: • KuuSh

JapaMala

Kampung Lanting, 86800 Pulau Tioman, Pahang Darul Makmur, Malaysia

Tel: +6 9 419 7777 **E-Mail:** reservations@japamalaresorts.com **Web:** www.condenastjohansens.com/japamala

Reached by luxury speedboat, JapaMala boutique resort is located on the unspoilt island of Tioman surrounded by 11 acres of vegetation framed by an inviting beach. Hillside and Jungle-Luxe Sarangs are in the heart of the rainforest and furnished in traditional Malay style created from natural materials. These luxury "nests" have spacious living areas and open air bath tubs or private hydro pools. The private, opulent beach-front villa, The Penghulu's House, is equipped with its own pool and boasts uninterrupted jungle and sea views. Savour true Asian flavours at Tamarind Restaurant or global cuisine with an Italian emphasis at Mandi-Mandi Restaurant built on stilts above the sea. Samadhi Spa is set on the cliff edge with one open treatment gazebo overlooking the sea and another located in a natural cave. Its Asian inspired menu uses natural Malaysian products and aromatherapy oils made from chemical-free ingredients, essential oils and botanical extracts. After a massage relax in the outdoor hydrotherapy pool with a home brewed honey-ginger hot drink while admiring the stunning vistas.

Key Treatments: • Couple's Massage with Essential Oil • Hot Stone Therapy • Coconut Milk Body Wrap
Key Products: • Natural, Biodegradable Products Using 100% Essential Oil Blends

SHANGRI-LA'S RASA SAYANG RESORT & SPA

Batu Feringgi Beach, Penang 11100, Malaysia

Tel: +60 4 888 8888 **E-Mail:** rsr@shangri-la.com **Web:** www.condenastjohansens.com/shangrilapenang

Shangri-La's Rasa Sayang Resort & Spa is set within 30 acres of lush gardens framed by ancient rain trees on Batu Feringgi Beach. Each of its 304 guest rooms and suites offers spectacular views of the Straits of Melacca or the landscaped gardens and pools, and is beautifully designed in a traditional Minangkabau style showcasing traditional artworks and handcrafted wooden carvings. The Rasa Wing provides the ultimate in luxury and features a private lounge and pool reserved for Rasa Wing guests only. Enveloped by walls made of local granite and shaded by the sanctuary of century-old trees, is CHI, The Spa, the first CHI spa in Malaysia; the largest and most opulent spa in Penang. With wooden and teak interiors, the 11 tranquil spa villas open out to the tropical vegetation. The treatment menu incorporates therapies based on ancient Asian traditions using locally inspired techniques and exotic Malay ingredients. After your treatment enjoy a dip in one of the resort's 3 pools whilst taking in the sea views or relax at the Pinang Bar by the beach.

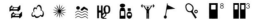

Key Treatments: • Traditional Full Body Massage With Herbal Pound • Moisturising Body Wrap With Cucumber and Aloe Vera

Key Products: • CHI Element Oils

HILTON QUEENSTOWN

Kawarau Village, Peninsula Road, Queenstown 9300, New Zealand

Tel: +64 3 4509400 **E-Mail:** queenstown.info@hilton.com **Web:** www.condenastjohansens.com/hiltonqueenstown

Hilton Queenstown hotel is located on New Zealand's South Island alongside the peaceful shores of Lake Wakatipu, just a short water taxi ride away from downtown Queenstown. Each of the guest rooms and suites is a serene haven with cosy fireplace and beautiful views of the lake and surrounding alpine village. The unique relaxation rooms boast calming interiors and private terraces with hot tubs offering the perfect place to unwind after a day exploring the great outdoors. The menu at the atmospheric lakefront restaurant Wakatipu Grill showcases the best of New Zealand flavours and is complemented by an extensive wine list with a keen focus on Otago's best winemakers. Be sure to pamper yourself at eforea: Spa at Hilton, the newest spa in Queenstown with a manicure/pedicure suite and 9 treatment rooms providing tranquil space for an array of globally inspired therapies, organic massages and results driven treatments followed by a dip in the softly lit blue-bottomed spa pool.

Key Treatments: • Anti-Ageing Facial Using Marine Algae • Invigorating Mineral Salt Scrub • De-stressing Massage Using Warm Bamboo

Key Products: • LI'TYA • Kerstin Florian • VitaMan

SPLIT APPLE RETREAT

195 Tokongawa Drive, RD2 Motueka, Tasman 7197, New Zealand

Tel: +643 527 8377 **E-Mail:** info@splitapple.com **Web:** www.condenastjohansens.com/splitapple

Split Apple is located moments away from the stunning Abel Tasman National Park on New Zealand's South Island. This beautiful boutique wellness retreat is built into a cliff face looking out to breathtaking views of secluded golden beaches and the Tasman Sea. Each of the 3 exceptionally spacious guest rooms is furnished in a modern Japanese design and features 2 private decks surrounded by fragrant gardens. The Fuji and Lotus Rooms boast 2-person granite Japanese bathtubs whilst the 2-storey Rainbow Suite has a separate lounge and bathroom with atmospheric LED lit shower. Relax and admire the views from the infinity pool and benefit from a personalised deep tissue or aromatherapy massage in the private treatment room. At the heart of any stay is the nutritionally tailored gourmet cuisine. The owner's passion for functional food that aids health and healing is reflected in the diverse menu prepared from delicious locally sourced ingredients. To ensure long-lasting effects attend a cooking lesson and book a medical consultation to attain a bespoke wellness programme.

Key Treatments: • Deep Tissue Massage • Apipuncture • Personalised Wellness Consultation With Nutrional Expert

Key Products: • His & Hers Beauty Products

THE PEACOCK GARDEN

Upper Laya, Baclayon, Bohol 6301, Republic of the Philippines

Tel: +63 38 539 9231 **E-Mail:** relax@thepeacockgarden.com **Web:** www.condenastjohansens.com/thepeacockgarden

The Peacock Garden is a boutique resort on the island of Bohol, set on a hilltop amongst beautiful gardens overlooking the turquoise Bohol Sea. All 32 spacious rooms and the opulent suite are decorated in traditional European style and feature bespoke furnishings and private balconies looking out to breathtaking sea and garden views. The exclusive Peacock Suite offers the ultimate in luxury living with a large lounge area and tasteful marble bathroom. Enjoy East meets West fusion cuisine at Old Heidelberg restaurant and drinks in the Wine Cellar. After a delicious meal retire to the Hemingway Cigar Lounge for a vintage port. Fontana Aurelia Spa is a Roman inspired, intimate sanctuary of relaxation comprising 6 air-conditioned treatment rooms and a private spa room with outdoor bathtub. Treatments are named after Roman goddesses and include customised facials, scrubs, bodywraps and signature 4-hand massage. After a treatment take a swim in The Peacock's focal point, the fabulous infinity pool, where you can admire the stunning natural beauty surrounding you.

Key Treatments: • 4 Hand Massage • Rejuvenating Red Wine Soak • Aqua Lily Sun Recovery Body Cocoon With Aloe Vera Body Polish

Key Products: • Pevonia • Locally Sourced Natural Ingredients

CAPELLA SINGAPORE AURIGA SPA

1 The Knolls, Sentosa Island 098297, Republic of Singapore

Tel: +65 6377 8888 **E-Mail:** reservations.singapore@capellahotels.com **Web:** www.condenastjohansens.com/capellasingapore

Capella Singapore is set on Sentosa island, a lush island overlooking the South China Sea, home to the world's finest resorts yet only 10 minutes from the city centre. The fusion of colonial buildings with award winning modern architecture is evident throughout the resort and the 112 guest rooms, suites, manors and villas combine contemporary Asian décor with pioneering technology. Many of the 1 and 2 bedroom garden villas boast sea views and private plunge pools. Choose delicious haute Cantonese flavours at the resort's fine dining Chinese restaurant Cassia, soak up the atmosphere of 1950s Cuban beach bar and savour a cocktail at Bob's Bar. Auriga Spa, named after a constellation in the northern hemisphere, is renowned as one of Singapore's best spas. Its unique holistic approach to wellness is inspired by the varying energies of the lunar phases. Signature treatments include massage, exfoliation and wraps using personalised products all in synergy with the celestial rhythms. Afterwards enjoy the herbal steam room or relax in the vitality pool overlooking a beautiful garden.

Key Treatments: • Seaweed & Eucalyptus Salt Scrub • Deep Tissue Full Body Massage • Lymphatic Facial Using Rose Crystals & Acupressure

Key Products: • The Organic Pharmacy • Own Bespoke Auriga Spa Products

THE SENTOSA RESORT & SPA

2 Bukit Manis Road, Sentosa 099891, Republic of Singapore

Tel: +65 62 75 03 31 **E-Mail:** info@thesentosa.com **Web:** www.condenastjohansens.com/sentosa

Nestled in 27 acres of lush clifftop greenery on Sentosa Island, overlooking the South China Sea, is The Sentosa Resort & Spa. A stylish retreat with low-rise colonial architecture and superb facilities, its 215 designer rooms, suites and villas feature chic contemporary comforts. 4 exclusive Garden Villas each boast a private pool. Spa Botanica, Singapore's first garden destination spa, features Asia's first mud pools, float pools with cascading waterfall and meditation labyrinths. Luxurious therapies are inspired by the rich botanical heritage of the region. Promising a refreshing destination dining experience, The Garden, located adjacent to Spa Botanica, presents wholesome, contemporary cuisine prepared with a gentle hand to retain the ingredients' natural goodness and flavours. A perfect complement to the entire spa and wellness experience.

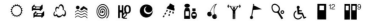

Key Treatments: • Singapore Flower Body Ritual • Five Elements Cleanse and Purifying Ritual • Mud Serail (Galaxy Mud Detox) and Massage

Key Products: • Spa Botanica Everyday and Premium Range • Aromatherapy Associates

REEF VILLA AND SPA

78 Samanthara Road, Wadduwa, Sri Lanka

Tel: +94 38 228 4442 **E-Mail:** bernadette@reefvilla.com **Web:** www.condenastjohansens.com/reefvilla

Reef is a beautiful boutique hotel set in tropical grounds overlooking golden sands and the iridescent Indian Ocean. The 7 exceptionally spacious and romantically decorated rooms are housed in colonial style palm-fringed pavilions. Each features tiled floors, an antique four poster bed and private veranda with Indian swing from which to savour the ocean views. Luxurious bathrooms open onto private walled gardens with waterfall showers. Begin the morning with yoga or take a leisurely swim in the beach-side pool. The helpful staff will be delighted to arrange a Champagne picnic, river cruise or customised day trip to the region's temples and tea plantations. For complete indulgence visit the small and intimate Reefresh Spa, where wonderfully aromatic exotic treatments using natural products are performed by the resident therapist. Afterwards, lie back in the outdoor bath beneath floating frangipani petals with a glass of champagne or king coconut water. As the sun sets on another perfect day, enjoy international and Sri Lankan cuisine alfresco beneath the stars.

Key Treatments: • Signature Massage With Sweet Almond Oil • Turmeric Honey Wrap, Salt Scrub & Facial Massage • Restorative Clay Cocoon

Key Products: • Locally Produced Natural Essential Oils and Products • Sweet Almond Oil

BANYAN TREE SAMUI

99/9 Moo 4, Maret, Samui, Surat Thani 84310 Thailand

Tel: +66 77 915 333 **E-Mail:** reservations-samui@banyantree.com **Web:** www.condenastjohansens.com/banyantreesamui

Banyan Tree Samui is set on a pristine white sand beach on the south-east coast of Koh Samui. Overlooking the sapphire waters of Lamai Bay, the 78 all-pool villas comprise of open-plan living spaces, luxurious bedrooms, outdoor salas and private pools. Built in traditional Thai style, villas are fully equipped with every modern amenity. The Spa Pool Villas include a treatment room, and the unmatchable Presidential Pool Villa features 2 pools and panoramic bay views. There are 3 signature restaurants: The Edge for all-day dining; the classic beach grill restaurant, Sands; and Saffron, for contemporary Thai cuisine. Using a holistic approach through blending ancient Indian wisdom with contemporary practices, Banyan Tree Spa Samui provides an extensive range of body and beauty treatments within 10 sea facing spa pavilions. The Rainforest, Koh Samui's only hydrotherapy spa, presents a range of hydrothermal experiences designed to complement each spa experience. After a treatment dine at the Spa Café for delicious meals inspired by the tri-dosha concept of Ayurveda.

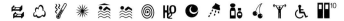

Key Treatments: • Invigorating Rain Walk • Signature Royal Banyan Herbal Pouch Massage • 4 Hand Massage

Key Products: • Banyan Tree Spa Exclusive Products With Fresh Herbs and Spices

CONRAD BANGKOK

All Seasons Place, 87 Wireless Road, Pathumwan, Bangkok 10300, Thailand

Tel: +66 2 690 9999 **E-Mail:** info@conradbangkok.com **Web:** www.condenastjohansens.com/conradbangkok

Located in the commercial heart of Bangkok, a short walk from the city's shopping and entertainment district, is Conrad Bangkok. Each individually designed guest room and suite has spectacular views of the Bangkok skyline and features the best of modern Thai design incorporating local silks and natural wood furnishings. For sheer luxury reserve the spacious Executive Terrace Suite comprising living room, bedroom and large balcony with sun deck and dining area overlooking panoramic Bangkok skyline views. More incredible vistas of downtown Bangkok can be enjoyed from the seventh floor rooftop pool. To unwind, savour a cocktail and listen to live jazz at the stylish Diplomat Bar and savour delicious modern Asian flavours at one of the 4 in-house restaurants. The ultimate urban retreat, Seasons Spa promotes healing and rejuvenation through treatments inspired by Thailand and Sweden. As well as 11 beautifully appointed treatment rooms, each with private steam room, the spa also has a fragrant garden and presidential spa suite, which is perfect for honeymooners.

Key Treatments: • Signature Massage Using Thai, Hawaiian, Balinese and Swedish Techniques • Revitalising Clay Wrap • Anti-Ageing Facial

Key Products: • Elemis • Pevonia • Erb

CONRAD KOH SAMUI

49/9 Moo 4, Baan Taling-ngam, Koh Samui, Suratthani 84330, Thailand

Tel: +66 0 7791 5888 **E-Mail:** kohsamui.info@conradhotels.com **Web:** www.condenastjohansens.com/conradkohsamui

Set on the island of Koh Samui on the Phang Ka Peninsula, Conrad Koh Samui is just moments away from an idyllic tropical beach and the blue waters of the Gulf of Thailand. The 80 ocean facing private villas are furnished in a blend of modern design using traditional Thai materials. Each offers beautiful marble bathrooms with oversized bathtubs and a stunning private infinity pool facing west towards the incredible sunsets. For superior luxury there is the Royal Oceanview Pool Villa with spacious indoor and outdoor living areas and a private massage sala looking out to uninterrupted ocean views. The resort's 5 restaurants include the fine dining Jahn where contemporary Thai cuisine paired with vintage wines from the private cellar is served. The spa is a complete wellness destination located on a dramatic cliff face at the highest point of the resort. Its 10 spacious treatment rooms feature a private deck where guests can relax before a holistic treatment from the extensive menu. After a treatment, unwind in the hot spa pool or savour a cocktail whilst admiring the sunset.

Key Treatments: • Full Body Exfoliation & Ayurvedic Scalp Massage • Body Scrub Using Organic Coffee & Essential Oils • Chakra Balancing

Key Products: • Aromatherapy Associates

PIMALAI RESORT & SPA

99 Moo 5, Ba Kan Tiang Beach, Koh Lanta, Krabi 81150, Thailand

Tel: +66 2320 5500 **E-Mail:** reservation@pimalai.com **Web:** www.condenastjohansens.com/pimalai

Reached by speedboat from Krabi, Pimalai Resort & Spa is located on the unspoilt island of Koh Lanta. This multi award winning boutique property is nestled within tropical rainforest facing a picture-perfect white sand beach. Spacious rooms, suites and private villas, some of which boast infinity pools, are all tastefully furnished in contemporary Thai décor featuring polished teak wood floors and Siamese artefacts. Private balconies offer spectacular vistas of the exotic gardens and unspoilt bay below. For the ultimate indulgence, stay in the opulent Pool Villa with rain shower, spacious salas and private pool with panoramic Andaman Sea views. 4 dining options include the delicious Thai fusion cuisine of The Seven Seas Wine Bar & Restaurant and fresh seafood at Rak Talay Beach Bar & Restaurant. The naturally inspired, tropical Pimalai Spa is a complete wellness destination consisting of 7 treatment huts and an open air massage pavilion. The Thai inspired treatment menu features therapeutic wraps, herbal scrubs and traditional massage using locally sourced ingredients.

Key Treatments: • Thai Herbal Compress • Thai Herbal Wrap • Traditional Thai Massage
Key Products: • Own Bespoke Pimalai Spa Product Range Using Local Ingredients • Decléor

SALA PHUKET RESORT AND SPA

333 Moo 3 Mai Khao Beach, Thalang District, 83110 Phuket, Thailand

Tel: +66 76 338 888 **E-Mail:** info@salaphuket.com **Web:** www.condenastjohansens.com/salaphuket

SALA Phuket Resort and Spa is a stunning villa resort set amidst coconut trees on the pristine Mai Khao Beach on Phuket's northwest shoreline. Its 79 stylish rooms, villas and suites include 63 signature villas with private pools and the palatial beach-front Presidential Pool Villa Suite; all room types offer abundant space and a serene atmosphere, open air bathrooms with outdoor showers or bathtubs, inviting day beds and salas. The exceptional beach-front restaurant serves fresh seafood and traditional Thai cuisine alongside international dishes; the romantic rooftop has panoramic views. For active guests, there are 3 large beach-front pools, the nearby renowned Blue Canyon Golf Course and a host of tours, excursions and activities that can be arranged. Set within an exotic garden, SALA Spa provides sheer relaxation in the comfort of 5 tranquil air-conditioned treatment rooms. The impressive menu covers traditional Thai massages and authentic herbal compress massages to indulgent body treatments, such as the aromatic sesame herbal scrub and water lily aftersun soothing wrap.

Key Treatments: • Traditional Thai Massage • Deep Body Hydrating Treatment • Asian White Clay Body Wrap

Key Products: • Clarins • Pevonia

SALA Samui Resort and Spa

10/9 Moo 5, Baan Plai Lam Bo Phut, Koh Samui, Suratthani 84320, Thailand

Tel: +66 77 245 888 **E-Mail:** info@salasamui.com **Web:** www.condenastjohansens.com/salasamui

SALA Samui is a stunning boutique pool villa resort located on pristine Choeng Mon beach on the island of Koh Samui. 53 of the 69 villas feature private pools with the remainder offering private balconies. Each is furnished in a stylish blend of traditional Thai and modern European décor equipped with indulgent open air bathrooms, inviting day beds and private salas. For the ultimate indulgence stay in the 2 bedroom Presidential Pool Villa Suite set amongst lush gardens; it boasts one of the largest hotel guest room swimming pools on the island. Dining at SALA Samui is a delectable experience. Choose from delicious international cuisine, fresh seafood and local Thai dishes at SALA Beachfront Restaurant alongside a carefully selected wine from the international wine cellar. SALA Spa provides a tropical sanctuary of relaxation in the comfort of 4 tranquil treatment rooms. Treatments include luxury facials and comprehensive spa journeys. Traditional Thai massages can even be enjoyed alfresco under the shade of the poolside sala.

Key Treatments: • Signature Massage Using Warm Coconut Oil • Signature Detoxifying Exfoliation • Thai Massage

Key Products: • Clarins • Dermalogica

EVASON ANA MANDARA - NHA TRANG

Beachside Tran Phu Boulevard, Nha Trang, Khanh Hoa, Vietnam

Tel: +84 58 352 2222 **E-Mail:** reservations-nhatrang@evasonresorts.com **Web:** www.condenastjohansens.com/evasonanamandara

Evason Ana Mandara is located in the coastal town of Nha Trang, on the south-east corner of Vietnam. A beach-front resort constructed in the charming style of a traditional Vietnamese village, the 74 rooms and 17 villas are either situated amongst lush tropical gardens or face fantastic views of the East Vietnam Sea. Inside, a contemporary design adorns the rooms and each features a private terrace, Jacuzzi and rain shower. For the ultimate luxurious seclusion stay in one of the beautiful Ana Mandara Suites. For active guests, there are complimentary water sports available at the hotel's private beach. And for food lovers the fine dining options include classic regional Vietnamese cuisine with an innovative twist at The Pavilion restaurant and a delicious Vietnamese Street Market experience of authentic flavours at The Beach Restaurant & Bar. The award winning Six Senses Spa offers guests a sanctuary for wellness and rejuvenation with an Asian themed treatment menu featuring an extensive range of traditional Vietnamese massages and more intensive holistic spa journeys.

Key Treatments: • Traditional Vietnamese Massage Using Suction Cups • 4 Hand Massage • Body Massage Using Different Massage Styles

Key Products: • Pevonia • Locally Sourced Mineral Mud • Traditional Vietnamese Herbal Ingredients

THE NAM HAI

Hamlet 1, Dien Duong Village, Dien Ban District, Quang Nam Province, Vietnam

Tel: +84 51 0394 0000 **E-Mail:** afomre@thenamhai.com **Web:** www.condenastjohansens.com/thenamhai

The Nam Hai is a stunning all-villa resort set on the pristine Ha My Beach. 3 UNESCO world heritage sites are nearby, including the charming town of Hoi An and imperial capital of Hue. Amidst lush vegetation, overlooking the East Vietnam Sea, the resort offers complete relaxation while reflecting the Vietnamese culture and warm hospitality. The 60 one-bedroom villas are luxuriously appointed with private gardens, outdoor showers and unobstructed sea views. The pool villas also boast a butler service. Savour exceptional cuisine at The Restaurant for inspired interpretations of traditional Vietnamese cuisine or fresh local seafood at The Beach Restaurant. Facilities include tennis courts, 3 pools, the Colin Montgomerie golf course and a kids club. The serene spa has been rated among the world's best; a haven of tranquillity. It presents a complete menu of treatments using pure botanical ingredients and follows the ancient healing traditions of the East. Experience a revitalising holistic facial, stimulating body polish or romantic bathing ceremony; all are intended to restore vitality and harmony.

Key Treatments: • Himalayan Warm Stone Massage • Detoxifying Seaweed Leaf Envelopment • 4 Hand Massage

Key Products: • ila • VOYA • Traditions d'Orient • Abahna

Princess D'Annam Resort & Spa

Hon Lan, Tan Thanh Commune, Ham Thuan Nam District, Binh Thuan Province, Vietnam

Tel: +84 62 3682 222 **E-Mail:** info@princessannam.com **Web:** www.condenastjohansens.com/princessannam

Set on the idyllic Ke Ga Bay, overlooking the South China Sea, Princess D'Annam is Vietnam's first all-villa boutique resort. Combining post colonial style with contemporary lines, the 57 exclusive villas are decorated with exquisite Vietnamese objects. Guests can take a leisurely swim in 1 of 4 stunning pools, enjoy various water sports or visit the many cultural sites nearby. Exceptional Vietnamese cuisine is served alfresco at the 2 restaurants. Built around a tranquil courtyard with shaded cloisters, the beautiful spa is a true haven. The menu offers an enticing selection of aromatic treatments using soothing natural ingredients such as honey, cloves, turmeric and ylang-ylang. Each therapy is personalised to the individual's requirements. For a particularly memorable experience try the Customised Marmalade Spa Package, which involves a body scrub and facial using mango, raspberry or guava marmalade, or book an Ultimate Spa Package for top-to-toe indulgence. Couples can savour treatments together in a VIP suite, followed by a glass of champagne in the Jacuzzi with ocean views.

Key Treatments: • Vietnamese Massage • Coconut Cocoon • Vietnamese Aloe Facial

Key Products: • Princess D'Annam Signature Scents from AZIAL

SIX SENSES NINH VAN BAY

Ninh Van Bay, Ninh Hoa, Khánh Hòa Province, Vietnam

Tel: +84 58 372 8222 **E-Mail:** reservations-ninhvan@sixsenses.com **Web:** www.condenastjohansens.com/ninhvan

Tucked away amongst stunning rock formations, accessible only by water and offering unparalleled levels of personal space, Six Senses Ninh Van Bay is the ultimate hideaway for those seeking seclusion. Here you'll discover a variety of thatched, timber-clad villas with muslin canopy beds, wooden tubs and glassy ocean views. Choose from Water Villas perched on the coral-bedecked bay to Hill Top Villas hidden amidst the trees. Spa Suite Villas - clusters of individual pavilions set into the mountainside - come with a butler, private infinity pool and spa room. Meals are exceptional: guests can feast on locally caught seafood whilst soaking up the spectacular views or may prefer to savour a barbecue from the comfort of their own deck. The Six Senses Spa is worth the trip in itself. Stepping stones pave the way through a moat to this heavenly sanctuary, which offers indulgent 3 hour treatment "journeys" and wellness packages in addition to signature Vietnamese therapies and wellness activities such as sunrise yoga, meditation, reiki and t'ai chi.

Key Treatments: • Reiki Crystal Facial • Holistic Massage • Traditional Vietnamese Massage

Key Products: • Signature Six Senses Spa Product Range • Sa Pa Essentials • Pevonia

VEDANĀ LAGOON RESORT & SPA

Zone 1, Phu Loc Town, Phu Loc District, Thua Thien Hue Province, Vietnam

Tel: +84 54 3681 688 **E-Mail:** info@vedanalagoon.com **Web:** www.condenastjohansens.com/vedanalagoon

Vedanā Lagoon resort & spa is spectacularly situated beside the shores of a secluded, serene lagoon; one of the largest in South East Asia. Within 67 peaceful acres surrounded by verdant mountains, this isolated, breathtaking setting is an oasis of privacy and exclusivity located between the World Heritage listed cities of Hue and Hoi an. The contemporary, fashionable architectural and interior design features characteristic Vietnamese touches, and each of the villas, bungalows on stilts and 2 houseboats are built from natural materials; many boast private pools. Dining options include the Horizon overlooking the picturesque scenery, the open air Sunset seafood restaurant and romantic Twilight. Vedanā wellness blends ancient healing wisdom from the East with modern practices from the West. The spa's natural therapies use Vietnamese fruits and vegetables, hand selected for their healing properties. Themed Vedanā treatment packages enable guests to unwind for longer; "romance for 2" packages are ideal for couples. Meditation, reiki, t'ai chi and yoga classes help restore inner balance.

Key Treatments: • Cupping • Foot Acupressure • Chakra Balancing

Key Products: • 100% Natural Products Using Locally Sourced Ingredients

Europe & Mediterranean

European spa culture dates from 12BC when the ancient Greeks and Romans bathed in thermal baths for physical rejuvenation and the therapeutic powers of water. Today, based on these ancient traditions, luxurious treatments such as hydromassage, Vichy showers, as well as sea salt exfoliations are available at many of Europe's exceptional spas.

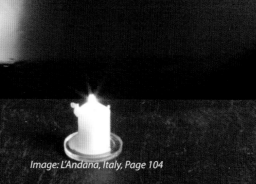

Image: L'Andana, Italy, Page 104

THE CLUB HOTEL & SPA, BOHEMIA RESTAURANT

Green Street, St Helier, Jersey JE2 4UH, Channel Islands

Tel: +44 1534 876 500 **E-Mail:** reservations@theclubjersey.com **Web:** www.condenastjohansens.com/theclubjersey

A small boutique style luxury hotel situated in the centre of Jersey's capital. Bohemia Restaurant is 1 of only 2 Michelin Starred restaurants in Jersey, and its hip bar is extremely popular. After dinner, while away the evening with a glass of wine or Scotch in The Club's trendy honesty bar, with its intimate home-from-home library setting. The stylishly appointed rooms and suites feature granite bathrooms, an abundance of natural wood and sumptuous duck down duvets and Egyptian cotton sheets. Begin your visit to the chic Club Spa with a swim in the salt pool. Thermal treatments, including the salt cabin and herbal steam room, will also stimulate and rejuvenate. The bespoke rasul room is particularly fun when enjoyed with a friend. After your treatment, retreat to the tranquil relaxation room or, in the summer months, relax by the outdoor garden pool.

Key Treatments: • Signature Facial • Aromatic Fusion Massage • Sea Salt and Seaweed Exfoliation

Key Products: • Darphin • CARITA • Clarins • Decléor

ARMATHWAITE HALL COUNTRY HOUSE HOTEL AND SPA

Bassenthwaite Lake, Keswick, Lake District, Cumbria CA12 4RE, England

Tel: +44 1768 776 551 **E-Mail:** reservations@armathwaite-hall.com **Web:** www.condenastjohansens.com/armathwaite

Armathwaite Hall is a beautiful 4 Red Star country house hotel characterised by charming old world hospitality, wood panelled public rooms and roaring log fires. The hotel is set in the heart of 400 acres of deer park and woodland, bordered by Bassenthwaite Lake and framed by the dramatic Skiddaw mountain and Lake District fells. Accommodation varies in the 42 individually designed bedrooms from traditional to contemporary and dining options include dinner in the Lake View Restaurant and modern Courtyard Bar and Brasserie. The Spa takes its inspiration from Armathwaite Hall's lakeside setting. At its heart is the stunning infinity pool illuminated by soft mood lighting and completed by an indoor waterfall. Spend time in the thermal zone's hydrotherapy pool, relax in the steam room or sauna or lie back in the outdoor hot tub and admire the garden views. After your treatments, unwind in the appropriately named Hush Tranquillity Room. Spa Day Experiences enable you to enjoy the spa's facilities at your leisure, or you might treat yourself to a spa break and indulge for longer.

Key Treatments: • Anti-Oxident Facial • Signature Organic and Prescriptive Full Body Massage • Organic Anti-Ageing Face and Body Ritual

Key Products: • comfort zone • Terraké

BARNSLEY HOUSE

Barnsley, Cirencester, Gloucestershire GL7 5EE, England

Tel: +44 1285 740 000 **E-Mail:** info@barnsleyhouse.com **Web:** www.condenastjohansens.com/barnsleyhouse

Surrounded by beautiful gardens originally designed by the world famous gardener Rosemary Verey, Barnsley House is a boutique country house hotel located in the pretty Cotswold village of Barnsley. Each of the 18 cosy bedrooms are uniquely decorated with contemporary British themed interiors and feature spacious bathrooms with free standing tubs and stone fireplaces. The Secret Garden Suite has private access to its very own English country garden. A delicious fusion of English and Italian flavours prepared from locally sourced ingredients and the kitchen's gardens awaits at The Potager Restaurant. And the traditional afternoon tea on the outdoor terrace overlooking the stunning gardens is a must. Housed in a separate dry stone building and enveloped by nature is the Garden Spa. Comprising 5 treatment rooms facing uninterrupted views of the countryside, the extensive treatment menu consists of indulgent facials and wraps as well as holistic massages and reflexology. Be sure to relax in the outdoor hydrotherapy pool and drift off to sleep in the soothing visual relaxation room.

Key Treatments: • Signature Full Body Polish, Aromatherapy Massage and Facial • Intensive Salt and Coffee Body Exfoliation • Reflexology

Key Products: • Aromatherapy Associates

CHANCERY COURT HOTEL, LONDON

252 High Holborn, London WC1V 7EN, England

Tel: +44 207 829 9888 **E-Mail:** SPA@chancerycourt.com **Web:** www.condenastjohansens.com/chancerycourt

Situated in Holborn, where the City meets Covent Garden and the West End, Chancery Court Hotel, London is ideally located for shopping and theatre-going. Set within a historic building, the hotel boasts some of London's largest guest rooms; all 356 rooms and suites are classically styled and inviting. After a day exploring London, head to the award winning day spa for complete relaxation. The Spa at Chancery Court is an Asian inspired retreat designed by ESPA. Treatment rooms are soundproofed and colour therapy lighting is selected to suit the guest's mood. Influenced by ancient Oriental, Indian and Thai traditions, therapies range from luxurious body scrubs and wraps to revitalising facials. There is a dedicated menu designed especially for male guests. As well as enjoying a specialised massage, guests might choose to visit the gold-leafed relaxation room, the perfect place to doze after an afternoon of indulgence. In the evening, the destination restaurant and bar Pearl awaits, with its exceptional contemporary French cuisine and tempting wine list.

Key Treatments: • Abhyanga 4 Hand Massage • Deep Body, Face and Scalp Massage Using Hot and Cold Stones • Personalised Facial

Key Products: • ESPA • Priori

CHEWTON GLEN

New Milton, New Forest, Hampshire BH25 6QS, England

Tel: +44 1425 282 212 **E-Mail:** reservations@chewtonglen.com **Web:** www.condenastjohansens.com/chewtonglen

Chewton Glen is a privately owned luxury country house hotel and spa located on the edge of the New Forest National Park, just a few minutes' walk from the sea. The 130 acres of beautifully landscaped grounds include a 9 hole par 3 golf course, practice range, indoor and outdoor tennis centre with resident professional, and an outdoor pool. Each of the 58 individually designed bedrooms and suites is decorated with sumptuous fabrics and rare antiques. Most rooms have private terraces and garden views. Vetiver at Chewton Glen, overlooking the gardens, offers a selection of menus and an exciting eclectic style of cookery. The award winning spa embodies the unique purity of both a New Forest and coastal location providing over 50 exclusive treatments in softly lit treatment rooms. In contrast to the contemporary treatment rooms, striking relaxation room and stunning hydrotherapy pool, is the 17.5 metre classical ozone treated indoor pool - the centrepiece of this lavish spa. After your treatments relax in the pool bar and enjoy a light buffet of local fresh produce.

Key Treatments: • Revitalising and Energising Facial • Deeply Cleansing Skin Specific Facial • Detoxifying Body Wrap

Key Products: • ila • Linda Meredith • REN

THE CONNAUGHT

Carlos Place, London W1K 2AL, England

Tel: +44 20 3147 7305 **E-Mail:** amanspa@the-connaught.co.uk **Web:** www.condenastjohansens.com/theconnaught

In the heart of fashionable Mayfair Village in London's West End, this exceptional 5 star hotel blends contemporary luxury with classic character; faithfully restored period features are juxtaposed with modern art and the latest technology. Guest rooms and suites are stylish and elegant, featuring bespoke furnishings and original art. Enjoy Michelin Starred cuisine at Hélène Darroze at the Connaught, one of the finest restaurants in London, a vintage champagne cocktail at the sleek Connaught Bar and afternoon tea at Espelette with its panoramas of Carlos Place and Mount Street. The Aman Spa is dedicated to holistic well-being. Inspiration has been drawn from ancient cultures and customs to create a revitalising haven and extensive treatment menu offering personalised signature experiences featuring the renewing and healing traditions of China, Thailand, India and the Americas. Each candlelit treatment room has a dressing room, while there is also a eucalyptus enriched steam room and indoor pool.

Key Treatments: • Signature Holistic Experiences • Osteopathy • Reflexology
Key Products: • Signature Aman Spa 100% Natural Skincare Range

CORINTHIA HOTEL LONDON

Whitehall Place, London SW1A 2BD, England

Tel: +44 20 7321 3000 **E-Mail:** reservations.london@corinthia.com **Web:** www.condenastjohansens.com/corinthialondon

The newest of the Corinthia properties, Corinthia Hotel London resides at one of the capital's most prestigious addresses, and its lavish interior and fashionable clientele live up to the hotel's glamorous surroundings. Expect the height of London luxury with some of the largest guest rooms in the city, their sweeping views and tropical rain showers being positively palatial. A walk-in wine cellar and private gym are just some of the amenities on offer in the Royal Penthouse. The hotel's fine dining Massimo Restaurant and Oyster Bar is the hottest Italian in town; be sure to try the home-made spaghetti with squid ink. ESPA Life at Corinthia is an urban nirvana of gigantic proportions. As the crème de la crème of city spas it delivers an endless treatment menu within its black and champagne marble and sinuously curving walls. Spanning 4 spacious floors there are 17 treatment pods, a Daniel Galvin hair salon, private make over room, 9 metre glass pool and for the ultimate in pampering, the Private Spa Suite.

Key Treatments: • Age Defying Enzyme Facial Peel • Ayurvedic Inspired Ritual • Rasul Healing Mud Ritual

Key Products: • ESPA

COWORTH PARK

Blacknest Road, Ascot, Berkshire SL5 7SE, England

Tel: +44 1344 876600 **E-Mail:** spa.cpa@dorchestercollection.com **Web:** www.condenastjohansens.com/coworthpark

Coworth Park, Dorchester Collection describes itself as a "hotel that rewrites the rules". It combines the warmth and elegance of a traditional country house with strikingly contemporary yet unmistakably English features. The 70 stunning rooms and suites in The Mansion House, Stables and Cottages feature free standing copper baths and original artworks; many boast captivating views over the grounds and wildflower meadow. Just 45 minutes from central London, near to Ascot and bordering Windsor Great Park, Coworth Park is set in 240 acres of parkland containing 2 private polo fields and an equestrian centre. The innovative eco-luxury Spa at Coworth Park is partially submerged into the landscape and built from timber structures with lime hemp. It is also the only hotel spa in the UK to offer Dr Alkaitis 100% organic treatments. Inside, the spa is flooded with natural light, and a modern décor creates a soothing, welcoming environment. After indulgent therapies, swim in the stunning indoor pool or savour a light healthy snack in The Spatisserie.

Key Treatments: • Luxury Diamond Facial • English Rose Wrap • Personalised Aromatherapy Massage

Key Products: • Dr Alkaitis • Carol Joy London • Kerstin Florian • Aromatherapy Associates

ELLENBOROUGH PARK

Southam Road, Cheltenham, Gloucestershire GL52 3NH, England

Tel: +44 1242 807 380 **E-Mail:** reservations@ellenboroughpark.com **Web:** www.condenastjohansens.com/ellenboroughpark

Nestled in the heart of the Cotswolds on the original Cheltenham Racecourse estate stands the newly restored Ellenborough Park country hotel. Comprising 62 bedrooms and suites, each features stylish interior design by Nina Campbell and spacious bathrooms influenced by the glamour of the 1920s, some complete with roll top baths; most rooms boast beautiful views of the rolling countryside. The Arkle Suite is the jewel in the crown with wonderful antique furniture, four poster bed and a private dining space. Adjourn to the Beaufort Dining Room for modern British cuisine against a backdrop of original Tudor fireplaces and beautiful stained glass oriel windows. And for more informal all-day dining enjoy unconventional British flavours at The Brasserie. The Spa at Ellenborough Park is an Indian themed haven offering indulgent treatments in 7 softly lit treatment rooms. Make time to relax in the tranquil spa pool and savour a drink at the juice bar. The global treatment menu brings together results driven and holistic therapies inspired by Africa, India and Asia.

Key Treatments: • Indian Head and Pressure Point Massage • Anti-Ageing Facial and Sea Shell Massage • 4-Hand Massage

Key Products: • Babor

LIME WOOD

Beaulieu Road, Lyndhurst, Hampshire SO43 7FZ, England

Tel: +44 23 8028 7177 **E-Mail:** info@limewood.co.uk **Web:** www.condenastjohansens.com/limewood

Lime Wood strikes a delicate balance between high luxury and relaxed enjoyment. Its 2 restaurants serve traditional British fare with an imaginative twist, with guests savouring the finest local organic "forest food" in the glamorous Dining Room and country house kitchen style Scullery. Main House accommodation ranges from cosy, spacious rooms with freestanding bath tubs and sliding partitions, to 3 luxury duplex Forest Suites with galleried sleeping zones and chill out area. 2 romantic Pavilions offer complete escapism; like private country cottages, each features a dining room, romantic first floor bedroom and terrace. The Herb House spa is a special place for pampering and working out with the latest equipment. Drawing on the forest setting, it features an expansive sauna with woodland views, a rooftop herb garden and Raw Bar serving delicious healthy food, cocktails and Champagne. The superb facilities further include a Mud House, steaming hot pool, Bath House with private indoor bath and steam room, and Bath Garden comprising a double treatment room and outdoor bath.

Key Treatments: • De-Stress Massage • Detoxifying Seaweed Leaf Wrap • Intense Smoothing Facial

Key Products: • Bamford Body • VOYA • NUDE • Tri-Dosha

LUCKNAM PARK HOTEL & SPA

Colerne, Chippenham, Wiltshire SN14 8AZ, England

Tel: +44 1225 742 777 **E-Mail:** reservations@lucknampark.co.uk **Web:** www.condenastjohansens.com/lucknampark

Lucknam Park Hotel & Spa, just 6 miles from historic Bath, is a beautiful Palladian manor house in 500 acres of listed parkland and gardens. All 13 suites and 29 bedrooms are individually styled with fabrics and antiques reflecting the building's character. Afternoon tea is served in the elegant drawing room or wood panelled library. The award winning restaurant, The Park, offers exceptional cuisine using the finest locally sourced ingredients. Within the ancient walled garden is the stunning Lucknam Park Spa. This stylish and contemporary spa features extensive facilities including the 20m heated indoor pool, indoor-outdoor hydrotherapy pool, outdoor salt-water plunge pool, experience showers and superbly equipped fitness suite. Before your treatments, experience the benefits of the thermal cabins, Japanese salt, aromatic steam, amethyst room, sauna and tepidarium. For complete indulgence, reserve a de luxe suite or double treatment room for your therapy. Afterwards, doze on a reclining bed in the relaxation room or dine at The Brasserie with open kitchen and wood-fired oven.

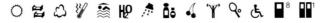

Key Treatments: • De-Stress Botanical Oil and Herbal Back Therapy • Pro Lifting Firming Face and Eye Treatment • Hot Stone Massage

Key Products: • Anne Sémonin • CARITA

LUTON HOO HOTEL, GOLF & SPA

The Mansion House, Luton Hoo, Luton, Bedfordshire LU1 3TQ, England

Tel: +44 1582 734437 **E-Mail:** reservations@lutonhoo.com **Web:** www.condenastjohansens.com/lutonhoo

Luton Hoo is a beautiful mansion hotel set amidst spectacular parkland. The hotel offers a host of delights and distractions. Play tennis on the restored Victorian grass court, enjoy the 18 hole golf course or while away the hours exploring the formal gardens and 1,000 acre estate. The 228 bedrooms and suites include classically styled Mansion House accommodation in keeping with their original décor; each has captivating views of the surrounding countryside. Nearby, the Grade II listed Robert Adams stable building and The Flower Garden are perfectly equipped and located for spa and golfing guests. Dining at Luton Hoo is always an experience, whether at the intimate informal Adam's Brasserie or the Wernher Restaurant. The converted Bothy building houses the spa, where you can unwind in the vitality pool or heat therapy suite. Signature organic treatments include the wonderfully aromatic bay and lemon body polish and wrap and stimulating 5 Senses treatment. Many therapies use exclusive spa blends inspired by flowers and herbs on Luton Hoo Estate.

Key Treatments: • Signature 5 Senses Body Treatment • Signature 5 Senses Facial Treatment • Hot Stone Full Body Massage

Key Products: • Signature Luton Hoo Spa Range • Circaroma

THE MERE GOLF RESORT & SPA

Chester Road, Mere, Knutsford, Cheshire WA16 6LJ, England

Tel: +44 1565 830155 **E-Mail:** sales@themereresort.co.uk **Web:** www.condenastjohansens.com/themereresort

Housed in a beautiful red brick Victorian building that dates back to the 12th century, The Mere Golf Resort & Spa is enveloped by an 18 hole golf course in the heart of the Cheshire countryside. Its 81 rooms and suites are all furnished in sophisticated contemporary style, in keeping with the building's rich heritage. Luxurious king sized beds with fluffy goose down duvets beckon you to unwind whilst the beautiful lakeside and garden views tempt you outside to explore. The resort's gourmet Browns@TheMere restaurant offers a delicious range of classic British flavours accompanied by a comprehensive wine list. For those seeking a sanctuary of wellness and relaxation, The Health Club and Spa is the perfect place to indulge in soothing spa treatments carried out in world class surroundings. Experience the benefits of the extensive thermal suite facilities including a hammam, caldarium, salt room and hydrotherapy pool. After a treatment, savour a light bite to eat or perhaps a glass of champagne at the Spa Lounge and Bar.

Key Treatments: • Anti-Ageing, De-Stressing Facial • Personalised Aromatherapy Full Body Massage • Hot Stone Massage

Key Products: • CARITA • Aromatherapy Associates

MODDERSHALL OAKS SPA RESTAURANT SUITES

Moddershall, Stone, Staffordshire ST15 8TG, England

Tel: +44 1782 399 000 **E-Mail:** enquiries@moddershalloaks.com **Web:** www.condenastjohansens.com/moddershalloaks

Moddershall Oaks is a lovely family-run country property in the heart of picturesque Staffordshire. With just 10 suites, an award winning restaurant and lovely spa it is the ideal place to escape and unwind for a few days or a few hours. The unusual Orient inspired suites are available for all-inclusive spa breaks or bed and breakfast stays; all feature a private deck with covered seating and some boast a spa bath and four poster bed. The lakeside restaurant serves creative English dishes using the finest seasonal ingredients. The Elemis spa offers the full complement of Elemis therapies as well as specialist skin care treatments and wonderful Ayurvedic experiences. The spa's focal point is the indoor pool complete with hydrotherapy technology and a relaxation deck. Lie back on the underwater airbed loungers, enjoy the invigorating sensations of the volcanic airbed or soothe away aches and pains on the massage hydro seats. Therapies can be enjoyed in the softly lit treatment rooms or book Exclusive Time to be pampered in the comfort of your suite.

Key Treatments: • Anti-Ageing Facial and Ice-Cool Thermal Massage • Lava Shells Massage • Shirodhara and Head Massage

Key Products: • Elemis • Aveda • Gerard's • SpaRitual

Park House Hotel & PH$_2$O Spa

Bepton, Midhurst, West Sussex GU29 0JB, England

Tel: +44 1730 819 000 **E-Mail:** reservations@parkhousehotel.com **Web:** www.condenastjohansens.com/parkhousehotel

A warm welcome awaits you at this charming family-run country house hotel located at the foot of the South Downs. The 21 en-suite bedrooms reflect a contemporary English country house decorated with antique furniture and inviting sofas looking out onto stunning views of the rolling West Sussex countryside. For a special occasion choose one of the 3 separate Luxury Cottages each individually designed with sumptuous fabrics and private terraces and gardens. The exquisite PH$_2$0 Spa provides an intimate and tranquil environment in which to unwind. The spa menu features a range of indulgent treatments including locally sourced organic chocolate rituals and the comforting hot lava shell massage carried out in softly lit treatment rooms. Be sure to experience the benefits of the dry floatation bed or simply relax at the spa's focal point, the stylish 15 metre swimming pool with stunning marble entry shower. Complete your day with a visit to Park House's restaurant to enjoy fresh seasonal produce taken from the hotel's Kitchen Garden and perhaps a glass of fine Sussex wine.

Key Treatments: • Personalised Facial with Eye Treatment and Massage • Chocolate Exfoliation and Body Cocoon • Hot Lava Shell Massage

Key Products: • Anne Sémonin • Aromatherapy Associates • Mama Mio

ROCKLIFFE HALL

Hurworth-on-Tees, Darlington, County Durham DL2 2DU, England

Tel: +44 1325 729 999 **E-Mail:** reservations@rockliffehall.com **Web:** www.condenastjohansens.com/rockliffehall

This exceptional resort destination is set in 375 acres of picturesque countryside. Most of the spacious rooms and suites in the Old Hall, New Hall and garden lodge houses overlook the beautiful grounds, championship golf course and River Tees beyond. Each of the restaurants, including the magnificent Orangery, has a unique style but all use fresh local produce. The stunning spa, one of the country's largest, offers a complete holistic experience and an extensive treatment menu. Work out in the state-of-the-art Technogym and Kinesis studio, join a Nordic walking class or experience the exclusive customised sleep programme. After a soothing therapy, relax by the spectacular indoor pool with stained glass windows inspired by those in the historic Old Hall, or enjoy the benefits of the thermal bathing suite. From the caldarium, infused with aromatic essential oils, move on to the salt room and finish by cooling your body with ice flakes from the igloo. Complete your day with a visit to the Brasserie for a delicious light meal and perhaps a glass of Champagne.

Key Treatments: • Sweet Pea and Rose Facial • Horse-Chestnut and Pine Scrub and Wrap • Signature Oriental Pearl Treatment

Key Products: • ila • comfort zone • Mamma Mio • L'Occitane

SANDERSON

50 Berners Street, London W1T 3NG, England

Tel: +44 20 7300 1400 **E-Mail:** sanderson@morganshotelgroup.com **Web:** www.condenastjohansens.com/sanderson

A truly special "urban spa" in the heart of London's West End, Sanderson offers a unique getaway from the hectic city into a world of tranquillity immersed in fantastical design. Philippe Starck has converted this exquisite 1950s building into a surreal Cocteau-like dream world featuring a landscaped interior courtyard garden, Suka, a restaurant by Zac Pelaccio and the extensive Agua Spa. In a place where innovative design is paramount, Sanderson's guest rooms are magnificent examples of pioneering style that captivate and enthral. The Agua Bathhouse and Gymnasium is equally impressive and practises an array of rejuvenating treatments that combine the ancient and modern philosophies. Enveloped in miles of diaphanous white curtain, the all-white treatment rooms, private relaxation suites and central lounge are peaceful, ethereal havens that ease away the stresses of everyday life. Experience one of the spa's 8 Inside Out programmes featuring specifically created healthly, nutritional spa cuisine that enhances the beneficial effects of your treatment.

Key Treatments: • Signature Facial Using Acupressure, Lymphatic Drainage and Reiki Techniques • Deep Tissue Massage • Hot Stone Massage

Key Products: • Eve Lom • Natura Bissé • Jurlique • NuBo

SOFITEL LONDON ST JAMES

6 Waterloo Place, London SW1Y 4AN, England

Tel: +44 20 7747 2200 **E-Mail:** h3144-th@sofitel.com **Web:** www.condenastjohansens.com/stjames

Sofitel London St James, formerly Cox's and King's Bank, is ideally situated for exploring London. The elegant accommodation combines traditional British design with unmistakable French flair. Sophisticated French flourishes appear throughout Sofitel So SPA, where guests are greeted by Fifi, the large French poodle topiary, before being formally welcomed by a spa butler who guides them through their spa journey. The stunning spa, bathed in natural light, retains original marble walls and decorative mouldings alongside modern contrasts like illuminated fret screens. Of the 5 stylish softly-lit treatment rooms, the Double Suite is particularly special boasting a rain sky experience shower and chromatherapy infinity bath. There is also a private hammam with traditional heated marble belly stone and bespoke steam shower room. After indulgent treatments, guests unwind in the deep relaxation room or savour tea and a delicious "macaron" in the airy and convivial patio within the old banking hall. Bespoke experiences include the Look Good Breakfast and Martini & Manicure.

Key Treatments: • Signature Exhilarating Massage • Signature Rejuvenating Facial Treatment • Aromatic Chromatherapy Bath

Key Products: • Cinq Mondes • CARITA

STOKE PARK

Park Road, Stoke Poges, Buckinghamshire SL2 4PG, England

Tel: +44 1753 717 171 **E-Mail:** Reservations@stokepark.com **Web:** www.condenastjohansens.com/stokepark

This magnificent 5 AA Star Palladian Mansion is the epitome of elegance. The 21 Mansion bedrooms and suites exude classical style with sumptuous fabrics and antiques, while the Pavilion houses 28 contemporary rooms and the spa. All of the marble bathrooms feature underfloor heating and cast-iron baths. Some rooms also benefit from spacious terraces with parkland views. The 2 AA Rosette Dining Room offers exceptional modern British cuisine with a twist and after a delicious meal, enjoy a drink overlooking the fountain gardens. The estate has some of the finest sporting and leisure facilities in the country and Stoke Park Spa by SPC is a tranquil retreat. The double height pool hall with 18m indoor pool affords garden views from its 20ft high windows; hydro seats are ideal for luxuriating between therapies. After your indulgent treatment lie back in an Italian marble steam room, cocoon yourself in a sumptuous duvet or unwind on one of the massage chairs in the relaxation room. Then sample a nutritious juice or herbal tea in the Spa Atrium with unique 5m tropical aquarium.

Key Treatments: • Collagen Age-Defying Facial • Hot Stone Massage • Detoxifying Ginger Scrub
Key Products: • Signature SPC Skincare Range

THE WYNDHAM GRAND LONDON CHELSEA HARBOUR

Chelsea Harbour, London SW10 0XG, England

Tel: +44 207 823 3000 **E-Mail:** wyndhamlondon@wyndham.com **Web:** www.condenastjohansens.com/wyndhamlondon

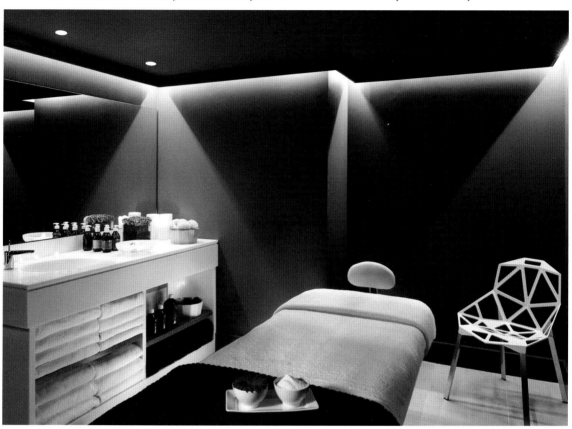

Wyndham Grand London is located in London's exclusive Chelsea Harbour, minutes from the fashionable King's Road and conveniently situated for exploring London. The city's only 5 star all-suite hotel, it offers an exceptional residential setting with marina and Thames views. There are 154 stylish, well-appointed suites and 4 penthouse suites with panoramic outlooks; each has a separate seating area, many have private balconies. The harbour-side Restaurant, Bar and Terrace Chelsea Riverside Brasserie is a unique contemporary dining experience; a British interpretation of simple but timeless dishes with the accent on the quality and purity of locally sourced ingredients. The Blue Harbour Spa is a comprehensive health club facility and indulgent environment for pure relaxation. Guests can work out in the fully equipped gym or take a swim in the invigorating 17 metre pool and try the soothing benefits of the integrated body and shoulder jets. Be sure to book the spa's signature treatment, a relaxing face, body and foot therapy.

Key Treatments: • Detoxifying Seaweed Wrap • Aromatherapy Massage • Collagen Facial

Key Products: • Aromatherapy Associates • Monu • VOYA

ASPRIA HANNOVER

Rudolf-von-Bennigsen-Ufer 83, 30519 Hannover, Germany

Tel: +49 511 89 97 97 00 **E-Mail:** hannover_mail@aspria.de **Web:** www.condenastjohansens.com/aspriahannover

On the shore of the beautiful Lake Maschsee, Aspria Hannover offers an extensive contemporary spa, comprehensive sports facilities and a wide range of activities, classes and one-on-one guidance from dedicated wellness advisors. The Restaurant and Bar were created with the gastronome and health-conscious guest in mind; cuisine is fresh, light and simply delicious. The spa's indoor-outdoor pool, lit by a warming fire, has uninterrupted views over the tranquil lake, while the garden features 2 sauna cabins. Guests also enjoy the whirlpool, foot baths, Banya and Turkish hammam. Treatment rooms, including the exclusive Partners Suite, have stylish Asian elements and the spa menu has a comprehensive selection of body and facial treatments. Guests can book an à la carte treatment, day ticket or day spa package. Overnight accommodation with direct access to the club and spa is also available. 20 modern rooms with extensive terraces bathed in natural light overlook the lake.

Key Treatments: • Signature Hammam Ritual • Deep Pore Cleansing Facial • Deep Muscle Massage

Key Products: • Decléor • SanVino

ASPRIA BERLIN

Karlsruherstrasse 20, 10711 Berlin, Germany

Tel: +49 30 890 68 88 10 **E-Mail:** berlin_mail@aspria.de **Web:** www.condenastjohansens.com/aspriaberlin

Aspria Berlin is a real escape in the heart of the bustling city, offering a tranquil retreat in which to unwind. Created for the ultimate in well-being, it combines impressive sports facilities, a magnificent spa and stylish urban hotel. 42 contemporary rooms and apartments enable guests to make the most of this extensive club. Set over 2 floors, the stunning spa features a range of heat and bathing experiences, from a biosauna, salt-water inhalation room and Finnish dry sauna to a Kneipp therapy area and plunge pools. There is also a beautiful authentic hammam. The spa menu comprises a variety of massages, body therapies, facials and beauty treatments as well as indulgent 3 hour spa packages. After their treatments, guests retreat to the quiet area with open fire or savour views over Berlin from the roof terrace. Enjoy cutting edge sports equipment, a 25 metre pool and personalised workouts provided by Aspria's team of experts. Activities include anti-gravity yoga, beach volleyball and bodyformer sessions, with personal trainers giving one-on-one tuition.

Key Treatments: • Lomi-Lomi-Nui Hawaiian Temple Massage • Aromatherapy • Micro-dermabrasion

Key Products: • Decléor • CARITA • Ligne St Barth

THE CLIFF HOUSE HOTEL

Ardmore, County Waterford, Ireland

Tel: +353 248 7800 **E-Mail:** info@thecliffhousehotel.com **Web:** www.condenastjohansens.com/thecliffhousehotel

Overlooking the inky waters of Ardmore Bay is The Cliff House Hotel, a sprawling glass-fronted edifice nestled amongst the rugged, heather-studded cliffs of the Waterford coast. A sparkling new addition to the pretty village of Ardmore, which houses the ruins of the 12th century St Declan's Cathedral, the hotel offers 39 light-flooded bedrooms with private balconies and bathrooms boasting egg-shaped baths in addition to several elegant suites which span 2 floors. Afternoons are best spent exploring the stunning cliff-top trails - Hunter wellies are provided - and come evening, guests can dine at the Michelin Starred House Restaurant where local ingredients are transformed into culinary art. Deep in the building's foundations, the Well Spa is a soothing space with a menu of indulgent facials and VOYA wraps using organic seaweed. Be sure to take a dip in the tranquil blue-bottomed pool although more adventurous types might like to brave the salty depths of the sea via steps descending straight from the hotel.

Key Treatments: • Detoxifying Envelopment • Organic Reviver Facial • Reiki

Key Products: • Anne Sémonin • VOYA

DELPHI MOUNTAIN RESORT

Leenane, County Galway, Ireland

Tel: +353 95 42208 **E-Mail:** info@delphiescape.com **Web:** www.condenastjohansens.com/delphiescape

Delphi Mountain Resort is a unique and inspiring destination where guests completely escape and unwind. Pack swimwear, warm clothes and sturdy footwear to make the most of your adventure. The resort stands before the stunning Mweelrea and 12 Bens mountain ranges, within 400 acres of Connemara forest and close to Cross Beach, one of the world's finest surfing spots. Full and half day activity programmes, led by professional guides and instructors, range from archery and hill walking to zip wire and kayaking. Delphi's restaurant takes local produce as its inspiration; lobsters and mussels are caught daily, and organic lamb and beef are sourced from surrounding farms. Delphi Spa uses only the purest, hand harvested and organic products; mountain spring water provides all of the spa waters. Holistic treatments include the detoxifying seaweed bath and award winning pear and green apple wrapcial. After an indulgent therapy, enjoy the thermal suite and admire the unmatchable views from the relaxation room.

Key Treatments: • Seaweed Bath • Signature Therapeutic Massage • Signature Facial With Mountain Spring Water, Fruit and Plant Pulp

Key Products: • VOYA • Éminence Organic Skin Care

FOTA ISLAND HOTEL & SPA

Fota Island Resort, Fota Island, County Cork, Ireland

Tel: + 353 21 488 3700 **E-Mail:** reservations@fotaisland.ie **Web:** www.condenastjohansens.com/fotaisland

Just 15 minutes from Cork, this hotel enjoys one of Ireland's most dramatic natural settings on Fota Island. There are activities for all ages such as Fota Wildlife Park, walking and running trails and championship golf courses. Rooms are contemporary and spacious, and penthouse suites boast a living room, master bedroom, balcony and high-tech entertainment system. Within the stunning grounds are 2, 3 and 4 bedroom lodges. There are 2 excellent restaurants: Fota Restaurant offers all-day dining, from buffet breakfasts to hearty dinners; and Amber Lounge serves lighter meals, afternoon tea and evening drinks, including over 75 whiskeys. The extensive spa has a beautiful indoor pool, hydrotherapy suite and Ireland's only walking river, which uses water currents and reflexology to revitalise. The treatment menu comprises over 60 therapies, some of which have been specifically created for golfers and active guests. After a therapy, enjoy the Acacia thermal suite with tepidarium and hammam or relax in a floatation bath.

Key Treatments: • Signature Face, Scalp and Body Massage • Marine Body Polish • Instant Lifting and Firming Facial

Key Products: • Kerstin Florian • Mama Mio • comfort zone • Les Lunéïdes

THE g HOTEL

Wellpark, Galway, County Galway, Ireland

Tel: +353 91 865 200 **E-Mail:** info@theg.ie **Web:** www.condenastjohansens.com/theghotel

The g hotel is located in the charming city of Galway, in the west of Ireland, overlooking Lough Atalia and was designed by Philip Treacy with his unique style and decadent furnishings. The Speciality Suites, including the sumptuous Linda Evangelista Suite, combine old fashioned Hollywood glamour with 21st century style. With vibrant jewel coloured interiors, Matz at the g serves locally sourced, contemporary seasonal dishes. Set in fragrant Zen gardens, the stunning ESPA at the g is a chic, Oriental inspired space with calming wood, mirror and slate interiors. Be sure to book a half or full day spa package in order to achieve complete serenity and nurture your body. Before the treatment, experience the benefits of the Rock Sauna and Crystal Steam Room or lie back on a heated lounger. After the therapy, guests may unwind in the relaxation room overlooking the secret bamboo Zen garden. Finish the day with a delicious bespoke g hotel cocktail in the hotel grand salon or the pink ladies lounge.

Key Treatments: • Dosha Specific Body Ritual • Purva Karma 4 Hand Massage • Chakra Balancing Treatment with Hot Stones

Key Products: • ESPA

KNOCKRANNY HOUSE HOTEL & SPA

Westport, County Mayo, Ireland

Tel: +353 98 28600 **E-Mail:** info@khh.ie **Web:** www.condenastjohansens.com/knockranny

Beneath the crepuscular silhouette of Croagh Patrick sits Knockranny House Hotel, a haven of traditional Irish hospitality and comfort in the west of the Emerald Isle. Characterised by its warm ambience with open log fires and thoughtfully chosen antique furniture, this Victorian style hotel offers 97 beautifully appointed rooms including 13 superb suites affording majestic views across the rolling countryside and breathtaking Clew Bay. Cuisine at La Fougère Restaurant is simple yet elegant with a menu showcasing the finest local ingredients and freshly caught shellfish. But it's Spa Salveo that really shines. A destination in its own right, this award winning sanctuary houses 12 spacious treatment rooms where guests can enjoy bespoke Kerstin Florian treatments, a Grecian style Vitality Pool and high-tech fitness centre. The jewel in the crown is the sprawling thermal spa suite with its mood enhancing Monsoon shower, salt brine inhalation room, scented steam room and invigorating herbal sauna.

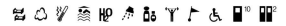

Key Treatments: • Dry Floatation Therapy • Serail Dead Sea Mud Therapy • Infrared Massage Therapy

Key Products: • Kerstin Florian • Mama Mio

THE RITZ-CARLTON, POWERSCOURT

Powerscourt Estate, Enniskerry, County Wicklow, Ireland

Tel: +353 1 274 8888 **E-Mail:** powerscourtreservations@ritzcarlton.com **Web:** www.condenastjohansens.com/ritzcarlton

In the grounds of the 18th-century Powerscourt House and Gardens, one of Ireland's most historic estates, The Ritz-Carlton, Powerscourt overlooks the majestic Sugar Loaf Mountain. Echoing the traditions of the country estate, activities such as horseback riding, fly fishing, cycling and hiking can be arranged close to the resort. After a day of sightseeing in nearby Dublin, strolling through the Estate's immaculately cultivated gardens or picture-postcard village of Enniskerry, return to your opulent suite. In the evening dine at the restaurant, Gordon Ramsay at Powerscourt, where an impressive menu of local dishes is offered with an equally extensive wine list. For sheer unadulterated indulgence visit ESPA at The Ritz-Carlton, Powerscourt. At its heart are the breathtakingly beautiful 20m pool inlaid with Swarovski crystal and the inviting relaxation area with views of Sugar Loaf Mountain. Soothe tired muscles in the state-of-the-art thermal suite and experience ESPA's wonderfully aromatic and holistic treatments and therapies. Why not treat yourself with a full day spa package.

Key Treatments: • Botanical Facial • 4 Hand Synchronised Massage • Warming Peat Body Wrap

Key Products: • ESPA

ASPRIA HARBOUR CLUB

Via Cascina Bellaria 19, Milan 20153, Italy

Tel: +39 02 452 861 **E-Mail:** info@harbourclub.it **Web:** www.condenastjohansens.com/harbourclub

Aspria Harbour Club is an exceptional retreat in the heart of Milan. The spa draws on traditional Roman practices combining heat and water experiences and includes an authentic Finnish sauna with garden views, traditional rasul and hammam. Spa Days enable guests to make the very most of their time here, relaxing in the outdoor hydrotherapy pool or aroma grotto steam room before savouring an indulgent treatment. The social heart of the Club is the renowned restaurant with lounge, extensive terraces and a classic Italian menu. The Club also offers outstanding year-round tennis facilities: 16 tennis courts on 3 different playing surfaces. Swimming enthusiasts will appreciate the 25 metre indoor pool and Olympic sized 50 metre outdoor pool surrounded by sun terraces and gardens. A poolside restaurant serving delicious light refreshments, an anti-gravity studio and a team of expert trainers complete the experience.

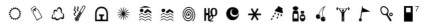

Key Treatments: • Rasul Massage • Caviar Firming Facial • Cranial Acupressure

Key Products: • comfort zone • La Prairie

L'ALBERETA

Via Vittorio Emanuele n° 23, 25030 Erbusco (BS), Italy

Tel: +39 0307 760550 **E-Mail:** info@albereta.it **Web:** www.condenastjohansens.com/albereta

An ancient vine swathed manor house in the heart of the Franciacorta Vineyards, L'Albereta is quintessentially Italian and truly exceptional. A privately owned boutique hotel, it boasts the ambience and personal welcome of a family home. Decorated in a romantic Provençal style, guest rooms feature antique furnishings and pretty fabrics and offer panoramic views of Lake Iseo, the Alps or green vines. The wines of the Franciacorta region are world renowned and ideally savoured with the remarkable cuisine of L'Albereta's Head Chef. The elegant Henri Chenot spa is bathed in natural light; an instantly inviting retreat for the pursuit of inner balance. Following a personal psycho-physical assessment, a programme of medical and cosmetic treatments is devised to cater for the client's precise needs. A dietician can also create a personalised diet programme. A spa break can last from 4 days to 6 days, but even a weekend visit will leave you feeling like a new person.

Key Treatments: • Anti-Ageing Therapies • Cupping • Reflexology

Key Products: • Henri Chenot

L'ANDANA

Tenuta La Badiola, Localitá Badiola, 58043 Castiglione della Pescaia (Grosseto), Italy

Tel: +39 0564 944 800 **E-Mail:** info@andana.it **Web:** www.condenastjohansens.com/andana

Deep in the Tuscan countryside on the cypress fringed estate of La Badiola awaits L'Andana, a rustic yet elegant retreat with honey coloured walls and sun drenched terraces. An original Medici villa and summer sojourn for Leopold II of Lorraine, Great Duke of Tuscany, this Italian idyll, brought to fruition by chef and hotelier Alain Ducasse, is understated luxury at its best. Florentine silks flutter in the pine scented breeze whilst floors are inlaid with antique oak parquet; stone fireplaces grace the hotel's 20 bedrooms, whilst the 13 individually designed suites are complete with Romanesque mosaic showers. Down in La Villa trattoria, dishes sing with Mediterranean flavour; try the orange flower brioche for breakfast or take part in one of the cookery courses and learn to bake it yourself. The indulgent spa is a slate floored haven of tranquillity with a mineral water pool, Turkish bath and invigorating ESPA treatments. Foodies will love the Gourmand Spa where delicate desserts and herbal teas enhance the experience.

Key Treatments: • Toning, Lifting and Firming Facial • Marine Algae Body Wrap • Exfoliation, Massage and Facial Using Olive Oil and Lavender

Key Products: • ESPA

LEFAY RESORT & SPA LAGO DI GARDA

Via Angelo Feltrinelli 118, 25084 Gargnano, Lombardia, Italy

Tel: +39 0365 241800 **E-Mail:** reservation@lefayresorts.com **Web:** www.condenastjohansens.com/lefayresorts

Lefay Resort & SPA Lago di Garda sits in 27 acres of natural parkland above Lake Garda. The central concept is the pursuit of overall wellness. Guest rooms feature decorative natural materials to complement the far-reaching lake views and boast high-tech gadgetry. The Lefay Vital Gourmet uses local seasonal products in wholesome Mediterranean dishes that tantalise the taste buds. At the resort's heart is the SPA, divided into 3 areas: bathing and heat, which includes indoor and outdoor salt water swimming pools and 5 different kinds of sauna; fitness, comprising a fully equipped gym and exercise studio; and the therapeutic garden, wellness path and running circuit. Couples can enjoy treatments together in the Lefay Private SPAs. The innovative, exclusive Lefay SPA Method combines the principles of Classical Chinese Medicine with Western scientific research. The extensive spa menu also has thalassotherapy experiences, Oriental rituals, massages and beauty treatments. Lefay's own dermatological beauty range uses medicinal plants and is completely chemical and preservative free.

Key Treatments: • Energetic Anti-Ageing Treatment • Acupuncure, Energetic Tuina • Reflexology

Key Products: • Lefay Spa Cosmetic Line • Thalgo • Charme D'O

PETRIOLO SPA RESORT

Località Pari - Civitella Paganico, Grosseto 58045, Italy

Tel: +39 0564 9091 **E-Mail:** booking@petriolosparesort.com **Web:** www.condenastjohansens.com/petriolo

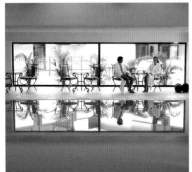

Petriolo Spa Resort enjoys an exceptional situation nestled amidst tranquil Tuscan hills. Its restaurants offer fine dining in romantic settings with soft lighting and ambient music. Before dinner, sample a glass of Tuscan wine at the outdoor bar and admire the beautiful grounds and panoramic views from its spacious terrace. The elegant guest suites are decorated in a classic Italian style with antique furnishings and boast private terraces. Within the resort's grounds are natural thermal baths where guests can experience the time-honoured activity of bathing in rock pools around the springs' source; the sulphurous water flows at a pleasant 43°C. Traditional and modern therapies are available at the spa to complement the benefits of the thermal baths. The spa also features 5 dedicated medical rooms. After an indulgent treatment, savour the calming atmosphere of the candlelit relaxation room.

Key Treatments: • Personalised Anti-Ageing Treatments • Seasonal Natural Facials • Craniosacral Massage
Key Products: • Own Bespoke Officina Benessere Products

TI SANA DETOX RETREAT

Via Fontana 5, 23885 Arlate - Calco (Lecco), Italy

Tel: +39 039 992 0979 **E-Mail:** info@tisanaspa.it **Web:** www.condenastjohansens.com/tisana

On the banks of the River Adda resides Ti Sana Detox Retreat, a destination prized for its prettiness as well as the fantastic health benefits it awards guests. An attractive farmhouse style building dating back to the 18th century, Ti Sana has been wonderfully renovated and now houses 22 luxurious suites, each with their own private entrance and Italian marble bathroom. Guests choose from an array of bespoke programmes ranging from a gentle 1 day detox to an intensive 3 week stay aimed to restore general health, vitality and well-being. The cuisine is based on a vegetarian philosophy with an emphasis on organic homegrown ingredients, whilst the energy enhancing Juice Fast is packed with fresh fruits and vegetables. At the heart of Ti Sana is the Galeno Medical Spa providing an extensive range of healing, health boosting treatments from hydrocolontherapy to ancient Chinese remedies. Medical consultations, nutritional support and personal training sessions are also available with activities such as hiking, canoeing and challenging golf in the stunning Adda Valley.

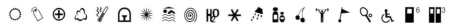

Key Treatments: • Detox Programme • Lifestyle Management • Personalised Holistic Experiences
Key Products: • Organic Moroccan Argan Oil • Pevonia • ANIKA ORGANIC LUXURY • PHYT'S

LONGEVITY WELLNESS RESORT MONCHIQUE

Lugar do Montinho, 8550-232 Monchique, Portugal

Tel: +351 282 240 110 **E-Mail:** reservations@longevity.pt **Web:** www.condenastjohansens.com/longevitywellness

Nestled in the green hills of Monchique, within a protected nature reserve, Longevity is a unique eco-friendly resort dedicated to wellness and prevention. Its extensive facilities include 2 outdoor pools, a beautiful heated indoor pool, fully-equipped fitness centre, and meditation lounge and deck but guests' well-being journey really begins at Longevity Medical Spa by La Clinique de Paris. Portugal's first medical spa within a resort, it adopts a fully integrated approach to preventive medicine and ageing management. Dr Claude Chauchard, one of the world's top specialists, pioneers a process of ageing management by addressing a number of contributing factors, from stress and diet to sleep and exercise. The spa features 3 different areas: Wellness and Relaxation; Beauty and Rejuvenation; and Health and Longevity. Cutting-edge programmes range from Slimming and Detox to Beauty and Health Optimisation, while packages can also be personalised. Longevity's healthy gourmet cuisine is based on Dr Chauchard's Vitality Nutrition programmes and uses the freshest local ingredients.

Key Treatments: • Personalised Antioxidant Therapy • Oxygen Therapy • Body Scrub With Sea Salts and Citrus Zest

Key Products: • Elemis

Palácio Estoril, Hotel, Golf & Spa

Rua Particular, 2769-504 Estoril, Portugal

Tel: +351 21 464 80 00 **E-Mail:** info@hotelestorilpalacio.pt **Web:** www.condenastjohansens.com/estoril

Guests have been visiting Palácio Estoril for its elegance, warm hospitality and stunning surroundings since the 1930s. Just 20 minutes from Lisbon, the hotel is set amidst immaculately landscaped gardens in the heart of the popular Estoril, enjoying beautiful sea views. 161 elegant rooms, including 32 suites, are classically styled and overlook the casino grounds and white sand beaches. In the evening savour fine local and international cuisine at the Grill Four Seasons before ordering a cocktail at Bar Estoril, once a favourite haunt for spies during World War II. Palácio Estoril offers a range of facilities: guests can tee off on Estoril Golf, one of Portugal's oldest and most iconic courses, or take a leisurely swim in the beautiful pool. For sheer relaxation retreat to Banyan Tree Spa Estoril. Taking a holistic approach to well-being, the spa offers a comprehensive menu comprising treatments ranging from Asian blend massages to indulgent facials. Signature treatment packages provide the ultimate spa experience; they include Royal Banyan, which features a revitalising massage using aromatic herb pouches.

Key Treatments: • Herbal Compress Massage • Rainmist Steam Bath • Pineapple and Coconut Scrub

Key Products: • Banyan Tree Spa Products

BARCELÓ ASIA GARDENS HOTEL & THAI SPA

Rotonda del Fuego s/n, Area del Parque Temático Terra Mítica, Alicante 03502, Spain

Tel: +34 966 818 400 **E-Mail:** asiagardens@barcelo.com **Web:** www.condenastjohansens.com/asiagardens

Barceló Asia Gardens Hotel & Thai Spa nestles amidst pine forest in one of the Mediterranean's most picturesque locations. Striking Asian inspired buildings stand in stunning gardens with free-form swimming pools (2 are heated), waterfalls and views over the Costa Blanca. Designer bedrooms reflect traditional Balinese style and combine state-of-the-art technology with ornate features. At 4 exceptional restaurants, authentic Asian flavours blend with regional and international tastes in delicious innovative cuisine. Activities include yoga and qi gong, bike excursions and golf tuition, while extensive jogging circuits wind through the grounds. For complete escapism a visit to the exotic Thai Spa is essential. Take a leisurely swim in the indoor pool, relax in the Turkish bath or outdoor Jacuzzi or lie back on the solarium terrace. The spa specialises in traditional Thai massages performed by its expert team of Thai therapists. For a truly memorable experience, reserve your therapy in one of the open air stilt houses with tatamis. 5 and 8 day Rebirth in Asia Packages offer complete well-being.

Key Treatments: • Traditional Thai Massage • Aroma Massage • Herbal Compress Massage

Key Products: • HARNN & THANN • Pañpuri

BARCELÓ LA BOBADILLA

Finca La Bobadilla, Carretera (A333) Salinas   Villanueva de Tapia, Km 65.5, 18300 Loja, Granada, Spain

Tel: +34 958 321 861 **E-Mail:** labobadilla.info@barcelo.com **Web:** www.condenastjohansens.com/bobadilla

Following the architectural style of the region's traditional palaces, Barceló la Bobadilla features a Mudejar style chapel and an impressive marble colonnade. Guest rooms are romantically decorated with Andalucían design, incorporating pretty floral fabrics and wood panelling. Gastronomic delights, including typical regional, national and Mediterranean dishes, are to be savoured at each of the hotel's restaurants and in the summer, dining is enjoyed alfresco. A wide variety of leisure activities are available, including horse riding and cycling – ideal ways to explore the surrounding countryside. For guests wishing to take things easy, there is no better place to relax than the 800 square metre spa, which comprises a heated counter-current swimming pool, hydrotherapy bath with ozone therapy, thermal deckchairs and Turkish bath. After your treatment, lie back under the gently swaying palms that encircle the shimmering outdoor pool.

Key Treatments: • Chakra Hot Stone Massage • De-Stress Oriental Chimes Massage • Holistic Facial Cleanse

Key Products: • Kanebo • Ecologic by Linda Nicolau

GRAN HOTEL ATLANTIS BAHÍA REAL

Avenida Grandes Playas s/n, Corralejo, Fuerteventura, Canary Islands 35660, Spain

Tel: +34 928 536 444 **E-Mail:** reservations@atlantishotels.com **Web:** www.condenastjohansens.com/bahiareal

Gran Hotel Atlantis Bahía Real stands in a secluded corner of Fuerteventura overlooking the clear waters of the Atlantic. The island boasts over 3000 hours of sunshine a year and a temperate climate. Reflecting the grandeur of the Mudejar palaces, the resort features colonnaded walkways with wide, open verandas and palm shaded courtyards. Most of the stylish rooms and suites have ocean views, while others afford colourful tropical garden vistas. 5 restaurants present a variety of culinary experiences and individually ambient settings. The Spa Bahía Vital enjoys panoramas across the ocean to the island of Lobos and offers extensive facilities. Take a leisurely swim in the free-form indoor pool with soothing sub-aquatic massage circuit, or visit the traditional Turkish baths. Later, sample from the menu of luxurious cosmetic and thalassotherapy treatments, body therapies and signature rituals before unwinding in the bubbling waters of the relaxation garden's Jacuzzi. Please note that admission to the spa is not available to children under 16 years old.

Key Treatments: • 4 Hand Massage • Traditional Thai Massage • Cupping

Key Products: • Cellcosmet • Natura Bissé

SHA WELLNESS CLINIC

Verderol 5, Playa del Albir, 03581 Alicante, Valencia, Spain

Tel: +34 966 811 199 **E-Mail:** info@shawellnessclinic.com **Web:** www.condenastjohansens.com/shawellnessclinic

SHA is a dedicated wellness clinic founded to help guests dramatically improve their quality of life. The 93 suites are instantly relaxing and rejuvenating. The Método SHA, fusing ancient Eastern philosophies with revolutionary Western techniques, underwrites all programmes from Weight Loss and Detox to Executive Health and Sleep Well; each tailored to the individual's needs. The healthy ageing unit addresses the ageing process and improves health using ultra-modern techniques. The aesthetic medicine unit uses innovative non-invasive methods. The extensive wellness facilities include the aqua-lab zone with therapeutic pools, physio-hydro massage beds, tepidarium and Dead Sea water floatarium. Herbal teas and medicinal herb-based drinks are served in the Tea Room with views of the Zen gardens. The superb cuisine is based on macrobiotic principles, enabling guests to enjoy gastronomic delights while also following a therapeutic diet. In addition, an à la carte menu featuring fresh fish and seafood is always available in SHAMADI for those guests not adhering to a diet treatment.

Key Treatments: • Detox Programme • Weight Loss Programme • Anti-Ageing Treatment

Key Products: • Aromatherapy Associates

GSTAAD PALACE

Palacestrasse, 3780 Gstaad, Switzerland

Tel: +41 33 748 50 00 **E-Mail:** info@palace.ch **Web:** www.condenastjohansens.com/gstaadpalace

Overlooking the Swiss Alps, Gstaad Palace is renowned for its timeless elegance and refined hospitality. The luxurious 104 rooms include 19 junior suites and the sophisticated 3 bedroom penthouse suite, while 5 leading restaurants tempt guests with a variety of fine cuisines. The Gstaad Palace Team will organise activities at your request, from river rafting in the summer to snow shoeing in the winter. The expansive Palace Spa offers extensive facilities and a comprehensive treatment menu featuring classic body and facial treatments and innovative new rituals. Every treatment is a memorable experience, but indulgent packages enable guests to unwind for longer and a private Spa Suite provides complete seclusion. The journey through the unique Hammam Experience takes around 2 hours, with 7 soothing stages progressing from a calming foot bath and cleansing soap foam body massage to a hydrating oil massage. Saunas and steam baths ease tired muscles while mountain views can be savoured from the relaxation room or welcoming lounge with roaring central fire.

Key Treatments: • Signature Hammam Ritual • Oxygen Therapy • Slimming Massage With Crème de Café

Key Products: • Cinq Mondes • Niance • L'Raphael • Sisley

Glossary

Be adventurous and inquisitive. Take time to peruse the treatment menu when you visit a spa.

Use our comprehensive glossary of spa terms to understand the vast and exciting array of spa treatments and therapies offered by spas around the world and how they might benefit you as an individual, physically, mentally and spiritually.

Abhyanga
Slow, gentle and rhythmic form of Ayurvedic body massage with warm oil. Aids detoxification and improves the immune system.

Ablutions
Washing or cleansing activities. Commonly performed as part of a religious ritual.

Açai
The Açai palm is native to central and south America. Its fruit is rich in nutrients and antioxidants and it is often used to prevent premature ageing.

Acrosage
Also known as: Inverted therapy. Developed by Benjamin Marantz. Combines massage, acrobatics and yoga and involves the client being suspended in an inverted pose from the therapist's hands or feet. With the head hanging freely, there is no pressure on the client's neck or spine.

Acupoints
The specific sites along the body's meridians through which qi is transported to the surface.

Acupressure
Also known as: Pressure point therapy; Pressure point massage.
Traditional Chinese massage involving stimulation of pressure points with needles or finger pressure to enhance the flow of energy in the body and relieve muscle tension. The therapist may sometimes also use their palm, elbow, foot or knee.

Acupressure facial
A facial massage that focuses on the manipulation of the 50 energy points in the skin and muscles. Relieves stress and improves and prevents wrinkles.

Acupuncture
Traditional Chinese healing practice based on Taoist philosophy. Fine needles are inserted into the acupoints.
See also: Acupressure; Electro acupuncture.

Acute disorder
Any severe ailment dramatically affecting the function of the body and/or mind.

Acu-yoga
A system of exercises combining acupressure and yoga techniques. Each posture stretches particular muscles and manipulates certain nerves or pressure points, releasing blockages in the meridians and re-establishing the healthy flow of the body's life forces.

Adjuvant therapy
A treatment given in conjunction with a primary treatment with the effect of enhancing the effectiveness of the primary treatment.

Aerobic exercise
Continuous rhythmic exercise (such as walking, jogging or running) that utilises the body's large muscle groups and raises the heart rate.
See also: Anaerobic exercise.

Aesclepians
An ancient Greek centre for healing.

Affirmation
Similar to visualisation. A positive intention or situation is deliberately meditated upon with the aim of refocusing the unconscious mind. Can be accompanied by recitations. Most effective when the body and mind are in a quiet state.

Affusion shower massage
Massage given under a warm, rain-like shower. Improves blood circulation.

African massage
An ancient healing massage, similar to deep tissue massage.

After-sun treatment
To soothe and cool the skin after prolonged exposure to the sun. The treatment might include a cold bath and a gentle massage with moisturising lotions, particularly of aloe vera.

AHA fruit acids
Natural acids frequently found in fruits. Often used for natural skin peeling treatments that remove dead skin cells and leave the skin fresher and visibly more radiant.

Ai chi
Combination of eastern and western methodology, including t'ai chi, shiatsu and aquatic exercises. Conducted in shoulder deep warm water, with slow, rhythmical movements and controlled breathing. Increases oxygen consumption, improves mobility. Deeply relaxing.

Aikido
Japanese martial art, focused on using the opponent's strength and energy against them.

Alexander technique
Technique developed during the 1890s by the Australian, F M Alexander. Method of improving posture and balance by focusing on applying the appropriate amount of energy for each action.

Algae
Products derived from mineral and vitamin rich marine plants. May be used as creams, body packs or bubble baths.

Algotherapy
Form of thalassotherapy using algae in treatments such as scrubs, body wraps and baths.

Aloe vera
Short-stemmed succulent plant native to northern Africa. Contains a significant number of amino acids, minerals and vitamins and is frequently used for the external treatment of skin conditions such as acne, sunburn and stings.

Alternative medicine
Treatments or therapies used instead of traditional or conventional medicine.
See also: Complementary medicine.

Amma
Also known as: Anma.
Traditional Japanese term for massage, deriving from the Chinese massage tradition "anmo". Amma techniques are based on Traditional Chinese Medicine techniques that are more than 5000 years old, and incorporate a wide variety of manipulations on the acupressure points. Dry massage through clothing.

Anaerobic exercise

As opposed to aerobic exercise. Involves muscular work that causes the body to use more oxygen than it takes in.
See also: Aerobic exercise.

Anapanasati

Meaning "mindfulness of breathing" this is the basic form of meditation thought to have been taught by Buddha.

Anthotherapy

Therapeutic treatments taking place in humid caves (from 30-42°C) or in dry caves heated by a hot spring to 50-70°C.

Anti-cellulite treatment

Treatment aiding body-contouring and cellulite reduction.

Anti-stress massage

A massage that focuses on key tension areas: the back, shoulders, neck and face.

Apipuncture

Chemical acupuncture with diluted bee venom originating from ancient Chinese practices mainly used for muscular pain.

Aqua aerobics

Aerobic exercise in water. The water's resistance helps to improve muscle tone and enhances cardio-vascular fitness. The body is supported by the water therefore is particularly beneficial for those with weight or mobility problems.

Aqua massage

Hydrotherapy technique conducted in specialist pools. Involves massage by underwater jets or a hand-held jet controlled by the therapist.

Aquabalance

While floating in warm 35°C water, the client is guided in passive and active movements by the therapist.

Aquamedic pool

Pool with water jets, which create a therapeutic and invigorating massage effect.

Arbutin

Derived from bearberry extract, this is a natural skin-lightening agent consisting of hydro-quinone and glucose.

Arnica

Plant with anti-inflammatory properties. Widely used as a salve for sprains and bruises, and sometimes for pain relief.

Aroma stone massage

Warmed basalt stones are incorporated into a full body massage with aromatherapy oils to further aid relaxation.
See also: Hot stone massage.

Aromatherapy

Aromatic essential oils are used in treatments such as massage, baths and body wraps. The oils are thought to have different therapeutic benefits, notably for the nervous system.

Asanas

Yoga postures or poses.

Ashiatsu

Derived from "ashi" meaning foot and "atsu" meaning pressure. A deep tissue massage involving the therapist walking on the back.

Ashtanga

Energetic form of yoga.

Aura

There is thought to be an energy field, the life force, surrounding the human body. This field is traditionally considered to be oval and comprising seven bands. The exact size, shape and colour are thought to reflect the individual's physical, psychological and spiritual state.

Ayurveda

Deriving from the ancient Sanskrit "ayus" (life) and "ved" (knowledge). The world's oldest total medical system, dating back 5000 years. Ancient Hindu science of health and medicine encompassing diet and exercise, massage and yoga. Propounds the philosophy that the best state of health is achieved when the mind and spirit are balanced in harmony with the body.

Ayurvedic massage

Massage performed directly onto the skin, with herbal oil, by one or more therapists. Loosens the surplus doshas, enhancing circulation and flexibility, and relieving stiffness and pain.

Ayurvedic shamana

See: Shamana therapies.

Baby massage

Massage performed on newborn babies to enhance circulation and relaxation.

Bach flower therapies

A holistic healing system founded by Dr Edward Bach. Plant and flower essences are used to enhance the emotional state.

Balinese coffee scrub

Exfoliating body scrub using finely ground Balinese coffee beans.

Balinese massage

Ancient technique, combining various massage methods, acupressure, aromatherapy oils and reflexology. Improves circulation and aids deep relaxation.

Balneotherapy

Traditional hydrotherapy treatment using natural spring and freshwater. Since antiquity, thermal baths have been used to revitalise and improve circulation. Today there are a wide variety of water treatments using hot springs, sea or mineral water. Sometimes a more localised treatment with a special hose operated by a therapist.

Basti

The introduction of an enema (such as herbal infused liquids, medicated oils or milk) per perineum (through the anus, the urinary passage or the vagina) to remove toxins. Can be effective in treating various digestive and metabolic disorders.

Belavi facial massage

Combines facial massage strokes, lymphatic drainage strokes and manipulation of the acupressure points with cleansing, exfoliation and hot towel wraps. Designed to firm skin and soften fine lines. Stimulates blood and oxygen flow and removes toxins.

Bikram

Yoga practised in a heated room (29-40°C) with a humidity of around 40%.

Bindi

Body therapy combining exfoliation and herbal treatment with light massage.

Bio sauna

A combination of humidity and dry heat. Gentler than a conventional sauna.

Bioenergetics

A system of body-orientated psychotherapy thought to enhance well-being by unblocking and re-channelling psychic and physical energy.

Biofeedback

A form of alternative medicine involving the measurement of blood pressure, skin temperature, muscle tension, heart rate and other bodily processes. The results are relayed to the client to enhance their understanding of the physical processes and means to control them.

Bird's nest facial

Also known as: The caviar of the East. The dried saliva of a species of swifts found only in the caves of the coast in Southeast Asia. The dried saliva is extracted from the nests and reformulated for an anti-ageing facial. Replenishes nutrients and improves micro-circulation. Particularly beneficial for dry skin. Skin is left supple and glowing.

Blisswork

Deep tissue technique which works on lengthening the tendons and muscles. Improves posture.

Blitz shower

Also known as: Jet massage; Jet blitz; Douche au jet. A body massage received while standing up. The therapist aims a high pressure jet of water at the client's body. As effective as a deep massage and stimulates circulation.

Body composition analysis

An evaluation of the percentage ratio of body fat to muscle.

Body conditioning

Any exercise programme that effects the overall improvement of the body. Often combines exercises for flexibility and strength and uses strength training equipment.

Body mask

The body is covered with mineral-rich clay, which is often enriched with essential oils. The skin is detoxified and hydrated.

Body polish

See: Body scrub.

Body scrub

Also known as: Body polish. Exfoliating body treatment using botanical or marine extracts. Mildly abrasive products are used to remove dry and dead skin cells, softening the skin in addition to improving circulation. Often used as a pre-treatment to massages or wraps.

Body sculpting

Fitness programme involving endurance training. Can aid weight loss and help shape the thighs, buttocks, hips and upper arms.

Body wrap

Also known as: Cocoon; Envelopment. The body is covered with products such as mud, algae, hot oil or cream and wrapped in plastic sheets or hot linens. Warmth enhances the cleansing and revitalising effects. Can be used to treat certain skin conditions.

Bodywork

Refers to various forms of touch therapy, including movement and manipulation.

Boreh

Also known as: Balinese boreh. Cleansing and exfoliating body treatment originally created by Balinese rice farmers. A paste of oils, herbs, seeds and grains is applied to the body. Circulation is stimulated and improved in addition to skin left feeling smooth and radiant.

Botanicals

Plant elements or extracts such as fibre, oils and juice.

Breema bodywork

Breema orginates from the mountains of Kurdistan and aims to create harmony between the body and mind. Combines various stretches, rhythmic movements and gentle touch.

Brine baths

Also known as: Salt water baths. A bathing pool of salt-saturated water. The water's high salt concentration allows the client to float and experience a sense of weightlessness.

Brossage

Salicylic salt and brushes are used for a fine body polish. Dead skin cells and impurities are removed. Skin is left soft and glowing.

Brush and tone

The skin is dry brushed or exfoliated, removing dead cells and impurities. This is a pre-treatment to a moisturising body mask. See also: Dry brush.

Brushing

Usually with a natural bristle brush, dry brushing of the skin involves long strokes over the body in the direction of the heart. Removes dead skin and impurities, stimulates circulation.

Buteyko breathing

Technique developed in Russia during the 1950s by Dr Konstantin Buteyko. Assists those with breathing related conditions such as asthma, hyperventilation, general breathing problems, snoring and nervous disorders.

Caldarium

The ancient Roman baths featured steaming hot water pools. Today, caldaria only sometimes have a pool of hot water, but all use steam heat. The gentle steam chamber has heated walls, floors and seats and aromatic oils can be infused to enhance the experience. Heated to 42-45°C. The steam has a detoxifying effect.

Campur-Campur

Meaning blending of varieties in Malay. A massage that combines both Malay and Thai techniques, and involves the use of a pouch of steamed herbs.

Carrier oils

Usually vegetable, seed or nut oils these are used to dilute essential oils before they are used on the body.

Cayce-Reilly massage

Highly therapeutic form of massage using castor oil and glycothymaline packs in manipulation of the joints.

Celtic Roman bath

A series of hot and cold pools, baths and showers, as well as steam rooms and heat experience rooms.

Centring

Achieving a quiet, balanced state by focusing on the hara (the energy centre thought to be located in the abdomen).

Chakra

From the Sanskrit meaning wheel or circle, and sometimes associated with the wheel of life. According to Hinduism, a chakra is a nexus of the human body's energy, qi, which flows between the chakras along pathways called nadis; there are thought to be 7 basic chakras, in ascending alignment from the base of the spine to the top of the head. See also: Chakra balancing.

Chakra balancing

Emotional and physical stresses can result in an unbalancing of the chakras, and consequently depression or a lack of energy. Combining the use of touch, essential oils, colour, sound and breathing techniques, chakra balancing helps to re-align the chakras and therefore restore the body's harmony. See also: Chakra.

Champissage

Also known as: Indian head massage. Head massage developed by the blind Indian therapist Nehendra Mehta.

Chanting

The repetition of a mantra. See also: Mantra.

Chocotherapy

The body is treated with cocoa and cocoa butter. Cocoa has anti-oxidant properties.

Choorna swedam

Powdered herbs are used to fill muslin bags to form boluses. These boluses are dipped into hot medicated oil and applied to the body. Soothes joints and eases muscular pain.

Chromatherapy

Also known as: Colour therapy. From the Greek "khroma" (light). Technique that dates back to ancient Egypt. Colour (in lights, fabrics, room schemes) is used to change the mood and stimulate the immune system.

Chi nei tsang

Ancient Taoist Chinese philosophy relating to the internal organs. The therapist works predominantly on the abdomen encouraging the internal organs to work more efficiently.

Circuit training

Exercise plan with complementary exercises and carried out on weight-resistance equipment. Aids stamina and mobility.

Classical Chinese Medicine (CCM)

Reportedly based on ancient Chinese medical texts, collated during the Han dynasty and thereby differing from TCM (Traditional Chinese Medicine) established during the more recent Maoist era.

Clay body mask

The body is covered in mineral rich clay and wrapped in thermal blankets. The clay detoxifies and cleanses the skin.

Coco de mer

A variety of coconut, unique to the Seychelles, with hydrating properties.

Cocoon

See: Body wrap.

Coffee scrub

Stimulating body scrub using ground coffee. See also: Balinese coffee scrub.

Cold plunge pool

Pool of chilled water in which to cool the body, particularly after a sauna. Stimulates circulation.
See also: Hot plunge pool.

Collagen

Protein responsible for the elasticity of skin. See also: Collagen therapy.

Collagen therapy

A fine needle injects collagen beneath the skin's surface to fill out lines and wrinkles. See also: Collagen.

Colonic irrigation

Intensive treatment. The entire colon is irrigated using warm water, removing toxins.

Colour therapy

See: Chromatherapy.

Complementary medicine

Therapies and treatments that are used in conjunction with conventional medicine. See also: Alternative medicine.

Compress

Cotton or lint pad usually filled with herbs or spices, warmed and pressed onto the body to relieve muscle strain and aid relaxation. See also: Thai herbal heat treatment.

Cosmeceuticals

Products that combine cosmetic and pharmaceutical ingredients. Used for improving the skin's condition and appearance.

Craniosacral therapy

Also known as: Cranial osteopathy; Osteopathy in the cranial field; Cranial therapy.
The craniosacral system is the membranes, fluids, nerves, bones and connective tissues of the cranium, spine and sacrum (the tail bone). Subtle manipulative pressure can enable the release of pressure in the cranium and body.

Crème bath

Treatment for hair and scalp. Rich cream lotion is applied to the hair. The hair might then be steamed before the treatment is rinsed out.

Crenotherapy

Steam, mud and mineral water are administered internally to treat disease.

Cryotherapy

Frozen or very cold products are applied to the skin to cause vaso-constriction. The skin appears lifted.

Crystal therapy

Crystals or gemstones are placed on the body to bring energy centres into balance.

Cupping

Also known as: Moxa ventosa.
Form of acupuncture focused on circulation practised for thousands of years. Oriental medicine states that pain or stress is due to the stagnation of bodily processes. The treatment stimulates the flow of blood, lymph and energy to the affected areas. Small glass cups are heated with a naked flame and quickly applied to the skin, creating a vacuum and drawing the skin into the cup.

Dancercise

Aerobic exercise incorporating modified dance movements.

Dead Sea mud treatment

Mineral-rich Dead Sea mud applied to the body draws out the skin's impurities. Often used to ease the symptoms of arthritis and rheumatism.

Dead Sea salt scrub

Massage using a mixture of water, essential oils and Dead Sea salt crystals. Removes impurities and dead skin cells, leaving the body revitalised and the skin glowing.

Deep-cleansing facial

The pores are opened to enable the extraction of blackheads and impurities and then closed, either by manual or machine assisted techniques. Skin appears refreshed and revitalised.

Deep tissue massage

Focuses on the deeper layers of musculature and muscle tissue. Deep strokes and finger pressure across and along the muscles and tendons release tension and increase flexibility.

Dermasurgery

See: Dermatologic surgery.

Dermatologic surgery

Also known as: Dermasurgery.
Performed by dermatologists. Techniques include the use of lasers, electrosurgery and the use of injectable agents.

Dermatology

Branch of medicine concerning the skin and associated parts such as hair and sweat glands. The skin is the largest organ of the body. Some skin conditions are an external manifestation of internal ailments.

Detoxification

Also known as: Detox.
Process by which body is cleansed of toxins and poisons. May be performed as a treatment involving applications on the body. May be a dietary change involving abstention from alcohol, smoking etc.

Din sor porng

White mud traditionally used in Thailand to address various skin problems. Thai herbs and yoghurt are combined in a natural scrub that cleanses and moisturises the skin. Ideally suited to normal or oily skin.

Do-in

Commonly practised in Japan and China. Programme of self massage, breathing exercises, meridian stretching exercises and chi exercises.

Doshas

According to ancient Ayurvedic philosophy, there are 3 fundamental energies or metabolic types (vata, pitta and kapha). Most people's metabolism is a combination of all 3 types, while predominantly 1 type. Thought to determine constitution, personality and sleeping patterns.

Draining massage

See: Lymphatic drainage.

Dry brush

Exfoliating technique. A bristle brush is used to remove dead skin cells and impurities. Stimulates circulation. Usually a pre-treatment to a moisturising body mask.

Dry floatation

Extremely relaxing treatment. The body is cocooned within a mud or algae wrap and lowered gently into warm water.

Duo-massage

See: Four-handed massage.

Ear candling

Also known as: Ear coning; Hopi ear candling; Thermal auricular therapy. The client usually lies on their side. A hollow candle is gently inserted into the ear and lit. This draws wax and impurities out of the ear.

Eco-spa

Environmentally friendly practices are central to the running of such spas; from ecological architectural design, to organic cultivation and water conservation. Clients may be educated in environmental sensitivity.

Effleurage

Massage technique of long, even strokes towards the heart. Aids blood and lymph flow.

Egg rolling therapy

Hard-boiled eggs are rolled along the body, settling hypersensitivity and calming the mind. Followed by a Thai massage.

Electro acupuncture

Acupuncture using low voltage electric current.
See also: Acupuncture.

Electrolysis

Radio waves or electricity are used to damage hair follicles and remove hair. Hair takes longer to regrow. May require pain relief.

Electrotherapy

Therapeutic stimulation with low voltage electricity.

Endermologie

Special form of deep tissue massage using a machine. Improves blood flow and lymphatic drainage and cellulite is reduced.

Energy balancing

General term used for treatments and therapies aimed at unblocking and balancing the body's energy flow.

Envelopment

See: Body wrap.

EQ4 meridian testing

Combination of therapies, including kinesiology, homeopathy and Traditional Chinese Medicine. A probe is used to test energy levels at the acupoints and determine which areas of the body require treatment. Certain foods and allergens are thought to weaken the body, these weaknesses being reflected in abnormal energy levels.

Equilibropathy

Focusing on the spinal column and related muscles. Modified form of acupuncture to relax tense muscles and regulate and harmonise the body's systems.

Essential oils

Fragrant liquids extracted from fruits, flowers etc. Used in massages and hydrotherapy baths.

Exfoliation

Removal of dead skin cells using mildly abrasive ingredients, such as sugar or salt.
See also: Brush and tone; Dry brush.

Facial

Treatment for the face. Usually includes cleansing, toning, exfoliating, massaging and moisturising.

Facial mask

Products, usually creams or mud, are applied to the face and left for a period. The pores are cleansed and skin softened.

Facial scrub

Exfoliating treatment for the face using products with mildly abrasive ingredients to remove dry and dead skin and to improve blood circulation.

Fango therapy

From the Italian for mud. Mineral-rich mud brine or oil is applied to the body as a mask or body wrap. Aids the removal of toxins and relieves muscular pain.

Feldenkrais Method

Created by Moshe Feldenkrais. Practitioners teach clients how to move freely and with greater flexibility. Can improve co-ordination, balance and posture.

Floatation therapy

Also known as: Isolation tank.
The body floats on salt or mineral water in an enclosed tank. Sometimes conducted in darkness or with music. The sensation of weightlessness is deeply relaxing.
See also: Dry floatation.

Floral bath

Bath enhanced with essential oils and filled with flowers.

Four-handed massage

Also known as: Duo-massage.
2 therapists work in tandem to perform a massage. Often combines several massage techniques.

G5 vibro massage

A vibrating machine is used to provide a deep massage. Fatty deposits are broken down, circulation is stimulated.

Garshana massage

Garshana means rubbing. Dry Ayurvedic massage using wool, cotton or raw silk gloves. Improves blood and lymph circulation, cleanses and exfoliates the skin.

Glycolic acid face peel

Anti-ageing facial. The glycolic acid is both odourless and colourless and causes rapid exfoliation. The skin's surface is smoothed and softened and lines are reduced.

Golden spoons facial

Hot and cold gold plated spoons are used on the face to open and close the pores, and enhance the skin's absorption of lotions or creams. Also improves circulation.

Gommage

Creams are applied in long, massage-like strokes to cleanse and rehydrate the skin.

Hammam

Middle Eastern variation of the steam bath. Hammams had an important role in Middle Eastern culture as places of ritual cleansing and socialising. Frequently referred to as Turkish hammam in the West as Europeans discovered the ritual from the Ottomans.

Hatha yoga

Form of yoga. Focuses on control through breathing techniques and asanas.

Heart salutation

Method of centring with closed eyes and deep, steady breathing. Hands are pressed together in a prayer-like manner, then brought to touch the chest, an acupressure point known as the "sea of tranquillity".

Henna

Natural plant dye used particularly in the Middle East to decorate skin with semi-permanent patterns. Usually part of ceremonial rituals.

Herbal wrap

The body is wrapped in strips of cloth which have been soaked in herbal teas.

Herbology

The medicinal use of herbs.

Hilot

A traditional healing practice from the Philippines, believed to be over 4000 years old. The treatment is customised to the individual, with the therapist working on energy imbalances and blockages.

Himalayan healing stone massage

Inspired by Tibetan healing rituals, hand carved stones heated in herb infused oils are used in a traditional massage. Restores vitality and balances. Alleviates stress.

Holistic medicine

Assessment of the whole person, including their physical, emotional and spiritual state. Followed by advice on achieving balance and well-being.

Homeopathy

Form of medicine that encourages the body to heal itself. Minuscule quantities of natural substances that effect similar symptoms to those of the patient's ailment are prescribed.

Hot plunge pool

Pool of hot water in which to quickly warm the body. Opens the capillaries.
See also: Cold plunge pool.

Hot spring

Natural hot mineral water spring. Sometimes volcanic.

Hot stone therapy

Basalt stones are warmed and incorporated into a Swedish massage to further aid relaxation. Cold stones may also be used.

Hot tub

Usually wooden tub in which to soak.

Hydrobath

Bath with water jets. Increases circulation.

Hydro-massage

Massage received in a bath fitted with adjustable hoses and high pressure jets. Stimulates blood and lymph circulation.

Hydropool

Pool fitted with stimulating high pressure fountains and jets to massage the body and relieve tensions. Sea water or water infused with essential oils might be used. Stimulates circulation, soothes aching muscles.

Hydrotherapy

Therapeutic treatments using water, including experience showers, mineral baths and underwater jet massages.

Ice room

Best used after the sauna or hot plunge pool to cool the body. Often with fresh ice to rub on the body. Strengthens the immune system and regulates circulation.

Indonesian massage

Ancient healing therapy more than 4000 years old. Deep, oil based massage similar to Ayurvedic massage. Deep thumb pushing techniques predominate as the therapist works along the muscles to stimulate the soft tissues and break down tight knots. Oil used for this massage is particularly therapeutic, benefiting the lymphatic system and circulation.

Infrared massage

Infrared massage devices use a combination of energy and pressure to break up tension within muscle tissue, improve blood circulation and reduce inflammation. The therapeutic effect can be enjoyed lying in a specialised capsule bed or by using a hand-held infrared massage device.

Inhalation therapy

Steam vapour treatment. Steam often enhanced with essential oils. Considered beneficial for those with weakened respiratory function.

Intonga Amasatchi

A deep tissue and stress relieving treatment performed with the hands and different sized wooden sticks to stretch tight muscles and reduce toxins.

Intuitive massage

The therapist responds to the precise needs of the individual's body.

Inverted therapy

See: Acrosage.

Ionithermie

Treatment may begin with a body scrub. A thermal clay and algae mask is then applied, after which pads are placed on the body, sending rhythmic electrical pulses to stimulate the muscles, combat cellulite and improve skin condition. Afterwards, the hardened clay is washed off. Treated areas are said to be noticeably firmer and tighter.

Isolation tank

See: Floatation therapy.

Jacuzzi

The free-standing whirlpool bath was invented by Roy Jacuzzi in 1968. Jacuzzi remains the trademarked name for the product.

Jari-Jemari

Herbal bath soak for the hands and feet. Followed by a scrub and massage. Relieves aches, improves circulation, reduces inflammation.

Javanese lulur

Luxurious Indonesian ritual, famous for its detoxifying and softening effect on the skin. Lulur is a traditional mixture of grains and spices, which is applied to the body.

Javanese mandi lulur

Meaning lulur bath, this famous treatment originated from Java. An exfoliating and body polishing treatment.

Jet shower

See: Scotch hose.

Kinesitherapy

Also known as: Kinesiatrics. Treatment that identifies physical and spiritual imbalances in the body through passive and active movements, massage and exercise.

Kneipp baths

Water therapy involving immersion in both warm and cold water to stimulate circulation.

Krauter bath

Powerful aromatic hydrotherapy bath using rich botanicals. Based on a German natural remedy.

Ku Nye

From Ku meaning "apply" and Nye meaning "massage". Traditional Tibetan massage believed to originate in the kingdom of Tibet over 3900 years ago. Body anointed with therapeutic oils. Range of kneading, rubbing and pressing massage techniques used. Believed to have both preventative and curative benefits.

Kur

From German meaning "cure". This is a prescribed series of spa treatments, usually involving the use of algae and herbs and particularly a programme of drinking mineral waters and soaking in mineral baths or natural springs.

Labyrinth

A spiralling path is traced on the ground or created using shrubbery. Walking along a number of circuits into the centre of the labyrinth and back focuses and calms the mind and aids meditation.

Laconium

Originating from the spas of ancient Rome, this dry and temperate sauna, with heated walls, floors and seats, is often particularly beneficial prior to treatment as it encourages the pores to open. In many modern spas, the laconium is close to a cold plunge pool or ice room.

Lap pool

Swimming pool with lanes. Usually 25 metres in length.

La Stone therapy®

A very relaxing, detoxifying treatment. Heated basalt lava stones and cool marble stones are placed on specific parts of the body, in combination with a massage using oil.

Lava shell massage

The therapist uses heated clam shells, known as lava shells, to perform a relaxing massage.

Lian gong
A set of therapeutic exercises developed in China. Gentle pressure is placed on the joints, tendons, ligaments and connective tissues to improve the posture and balance and to combat stress.

Liquid sound
A special sound system playing soothing music underwater.

Lomi lomi
Also known as: Kahuna massage; Lomilomi; Loving hands, Lomi-Lomi-Nui Hawaiian. Traditional technique created by the ancient Polynesians. Sometimes referred to as "loving hands" because of the continuous, gentle strokes. May incorporate traditional healing prayers or rituals.

Loofah scrub
The mildly abrasive, sponge-like skeleton of the loofah, a gourd family vegetable, is used for exfoliation.

Luk pra kob
A traditional Thai hot compress massage. Blend of herbs including turmeric, tamarind, lemongrass and Kaffir lime are wrapped in cotton and steamed. Soothes and relieves muscular pain and inflammation. Nourishes the skin.

Lymphatic drainage
Also known as: Draining massage.
A form of massage using undulating strokes to stimulate lymphatic circulation, reduce fluid retention and clear trapped toxins. Often undertaken as an adjunct to a slimming programme.

Macrobiotics
From the Greek "macro" (long) and "bios" (life) a theory of promoting health and longevity by means of diet, principally focussed on whole grains and beans.

Massage
Traditional massage using long kneading strokes and pressure. May be performed with hot oil.

Mandi lulur
See: Javanese lulur.

Manicure
Largely aesthetic treatment for hands and nails. May also include a hand massage.

Mantra
Syllable or phrase repeated to focus the mind. Use originated in the Indian Vedic religion, later a fundamental aspect of Hinduism, Sikhism, Buddhism and Jainism.
See also: Chanting.

Manuluve
Treatment for the hands and arms, including a scrub and massage using heated seaweed.

Marine aerosol treatment
Sea water steam is inhaled to cleanse the airways and alleviate breathing problems.

Marma point massage
Ayurvedic massage. The thumbs or index fingers massage the marma points in circular motions. Focuses on scalp, face, neck and shoulders.

Marma points
According to Ayurveda, these are the body's energy points. Dysfunction at these points is thought to be the cause of illness.

Masanuga therapy
See: Zen shiatsu.

Massage
Manipulative technique used on the tissues. Usually performed by hand, but water jets and machines can also be used. Improves blood circulation and the digestive system, encourages the removal of toxins from the body, eases muscle strain and relaxes.

Masseur
Male massage therapist.

Masseuse
Female massage therapist.

Maya Therapy
Abdominal massage technique based on the Mayan philosophy originating from Central American spiritual healers in the pre-classic period (c. 2000 BC to 250 AD). When applied, the Mayan abdominal therapy techniques guide internal abdominal organs into their correct position for optimum health and well-being. Particularly beneficial for women as it can correct a displaced or prolapsed uterus and or bladder.

Meditation
Method of contemplation involving deep breathing. During meditation, breathing, heart rate and pulse slow. Relieves stress, reduces blood pressure, leads to a greater sense of inner calm.

Melukat
According to Malay tradition, a bride and groom would be kept in their family homes for 3 days before their wedding. Their mothers would prepare them for their wedding by performing the traditional melukat or body cleansing.

Meridian
Pathways through which energy flows around the body. Illnesses are thought to be caused by blockages in these pathways.

Meridian shiatsu
Derivative form of shiatsu, focused on the principle of meridians.
See also: Shiatsu; Zen shiatsu.

Meridian-stretching
Combination of TMC (Traditional Chinese Medicine), yoga and exercises, designed to enhance physical and mental flexibility.

Mesipat
A traditional Balinese facial using local herbs, sandalwood and tamarind leaves.

Metabolism
Rate at which the body converts fuel into energy.

Micro-dermabrasion
Facial exfoliation. The skin is blasted with very fine aluminium oxide crystals to remove dead skin. Skin is left smooth and glowing.

Moor mud or peat baths
Mineral rich mud from a moor or peat marsh is used in a bath to exfoliate and hydrate the skin. Also has anti-inflammatory properties.

Moxa ventosa
See: Cupping.

Moxibustion
The dried herb moxa is burned above the acupoints to alleviate pain.

Mud pool
Volcanic mud is self-applied to the body and allowed to dry before being rinsed off. Cleanses the skin.

Mud serail
Mineral rich mud is self-applied in a steam room. After a short time it is rinsed off. The muscles are warmed and soothed, the skin is cleansed.

Mukhabhyanga
Ayurvedic face massage. Relaxes the facial muscles and stimulates blood and lymph flow.

Mukhalepam
Also known as: Mukhalepanam.
From Mukham meaning face and lepa, lepana or lepanam meaning the application of paste. Simple Ayurvedic skin care therapy. Freshly prepared herbal face mask is applied to the face and massaged away after 30-45 mins. Believed to have anti-ageing benefits. Can prove beneficial in treating sun burn.

Nasya
Use of medicated solution in the nasal passages to help alleviate allergies. One of the 5 purification techniques of Panchakarma.

Naturotherapy

Also known as: Natural medicine.
Holistic approach based on the belief that the body can heal itself. Treatments encourage self-healing, rather than alleviating symptoms.

Neutraceuticals

Foodstuffs fortified with vitamins, minerals, herbs and other supplements to boost health.

Njavarakizhi

Ayurvedic massage. Linen bags filled with rice cooked in milk and infused with herbs applied to the body with medicated oil. Induces sweat.

Obsidian stone massage

Massage using Obsidian, a form of volcanic rock formed when lava cools quickly.
See also: Hot stone therapy.

Onsen

Natural hot springs (Japanese).

Osteopathy

An alternative medicine based on the belief in the body's ability to heal itself. Osteopaths have a holistic approach and believe that the whole body will work well if it is in good structural balance. Treatment involves gentle manipulation to release tension, stretching muscles and relieving pain. Most commonly used for treating back and neck pain.

Oxygen facial

Treatment comprising nutrients and oxygen is sprayed onto or applied to the face. Thought to relieve the signs of ageing.

Oxygen therapy

Treatment that increases the supply of oxygen to the lungs, tissues and organs in order to promote healing and improve health.

Ozone Bath

Jets of ozone bubbles are directed onto the body, which is immersed in thermal or salt water. Stimulates the circulation.

Padabhyanga

Ayurvedic massage focusing on the legs and feet. Improves circulation and can be used to treat or prevent varicose veins.

Panchakarma

Ayurvedic treatment to rid the body of toxins. May involve massage, yoga and sweat therapy.

Parafango

Volcanic mud mixed with paraffin wax is brushed over the body. Alleviates aches and pains.

Paraffin treatment

Warm paraffin wax is applied to the hands and feet to absorb toxins and smooth the skin.

Patra podala swedenam

Curative herbs and leaves fried in medicated oil are applied to the body during a full massage.

Pedicure

Beauty treatment for the feet and toenails. The feet are soaked and exfoliated. The toenails are trimmed, shaped and possibly painted with nail polish. May also incorporate a foot massage.

Pedilave

The feet and legs are dipped in alternate vessels of hot and cold water to stimulate blood circulation.

Pelotherapy

Mud wraps or baths are used to treat skin or digestive ailments and rheumatism.

Physiotherapy

Rehabilitation therapy to aid recovery from injury, disease or surgery. Treatments include hydrotherapy and massage, and relieve pain as well as promoting healing and improving strength.

Phytotherapy

Also known as: Herbal medicine.
Use of plants, such as seaweed and herbs, for medicinal purposes in conjunction with wraps, massage and steam and inhalation therapies.

Pilates

Programme developed by Joseph Pilates aimed at conditioning the body through a series of controlled movements. Uses specially designed equipment to enhance strength and flexibility.

Pizhichil

Ayurvedic massage. Gentle application of herbal oil to the body by 2 or 4 therapists.

Polarity massage

Treatment involving stretching, gentle rocking and the placing of hands along the meridians to balance the body's energy.

Poultice

A paste is spread onto cloth, or between layers of cloth.

Power yoga

Energetic form of yoga. Stretches and strengthens the muscles.

Pranayama

Modes of breathing control in yoga.

Pressure point massage

See: Acupressure.

Primordial sound meditation

Ancient technique which is practised in silence. A personal sound mantra is adopted and used to enhance relaxation and visualisation.

Pristhabhyanga

Ayurvedic back massage. Herb-infused oils are applied with a massage to relax the muscles, improve blood circulation and promote energy flow.

Purvakarma

Combining 2 treatments, anehana and svedana, to prepare the skin before panchakarma.

Qi

Also known as: Ki (Japanese); Prana (Indian); Sên (Thai).
The life force or energy in the body (Chinese).

Qi gong

Series of Chinese self-healing exercises. Breathing and simple movements are used together with visualisation to control the qi and strengthen the mind and body.

Rasul

Traditional Arabian cleansing ritual. Mineral-rich mud is self-applied in a special steam room, which may be filled with aromatic infused steam. The mud is then rinsed off leaving the skin thoroughly cleansed and detoxified.

Rattan Tapping

Rattan sticks are gently tapped against the body as part of a qi gong massage.

Reflexology

Ancient Chinese practice. Acupoint massage is applied to the feet, and sometimes to the hands and ears, to re-establish the body's energy flow. Specific parts of the feet and hands correspond with other body parts of the body. Their manipulation can effect associated change. Improves circulation and relaxes.

Reiki

Holistic healing art based on ancient Tibetan teachings and reintroduced in the mid 19th century in Japan by Dr Mikao Usui. "Reiki" in Japanese means universal life force energy. Hands are laid on or above the body to energise and aid healing.

Repaichage

Body treatment using mud, clay, seaweed and herbs to cleanse and moisturise the skin.

Restorative yoga

A passive form of yoga. Supported by cushions, you are gently guided by a practitioner. By releasing tension in the spine and muscles, the technique relaxes the body and rejuvenates the mind. This does not require as much flexibility as other forms of yoga.

Rolfing structural engineering

A massage system that manipulates the body's muscular-skeletal system. Aims to realign the body structurally and improve the posture.

Roman bath

The baths of ancient Rome incorporated a series of hot, warm and cold pools.

Salt glow

Also known as: Salt scrub.
Exfoliant of coarse salt, sometimes fused with essential oils, is applied to the body.

Samana

Ayurvedic herbal medicine thought to balance the doshas.

Sanus per aquam

Also known as: Salus per aquam.
It is often argued that the word SPA is an acronym for the Roman sanus per aquam, meaning health or healing through water.

Sauna

Heated wooden treatment room. The heat causes sweating, which cleanses the body of impurities and relaxes the muscles. Combined with cold showers, sauna therapy is thought to relieve stress and enhance the immune system.

Scotch hose

A high pressure hose of alternate hot and cold water is directed at the standing client. Stimulates circulation and relieves muscle tension. Fresh or salt water may be used.

Seaweed wrap

A mixture of seawater and seaweed is applied to the body, which is then wrapped. Detoxifies the skin. Can improve the appearance of cellulite.

Shamana therapies

Also known as: Ayurvedic shamana; Shamana.
From the word shamana meaning suppress or balance. A palliative therapy, which addresses the imbalance of humours or doshas through the use of customised diets and exercise.

Shiatsu

Japanese massage technique. Finger pressure is used to stimulate and unblock the meridians.

Shirobhyanga

Ayurvedic face massage. Relaxes the face muscles and stimulates the circulation.

Shirodhara

Also known as: Sirodhara.
Ayurvedic treatment. A steady stream of fragrant medicated oil is poured onto the third eye in the centre of the forehead. Improves concentration and relieves tension. Deeply relaxing.

Shirovasthi

Ayurvedic treatment. Warm, herbal oil is massaged onto the head. A cap is worn for a while to retain the beneficial effects of the treatment.

Signature treatment

A treatment created by a particular spa or spa brand.

Silk foulard

A silk scarf is used in certain massages with some light pressure and stretching techniques.

Sitz bath

The lower half of the body is immersed in warm herbal water within an upright bath. The feet are soaked alternately in hot and cold water in order to stimulate the immune system.

Sivananda

Form of yoga comprising 12 sun salutation poses.

Slenisium body wrap

Natural oils are applied to the skin. The body is then wrapped in cloth, encouraging the elimination of toxins and excess fluid from the body.

Snehana

An Ayurvedic therapy using a mixture of oil, herbs and other natural products when massaging the body. Sometimes oils may also be ingested or introduced as enemas. One of the preparatory treatments for purvakarma.

Spa cuisine

Light, fresh and healthy meals served in spas to enhance well-being.

Spinning

Indoor cycling on stationary bikes with adjustable resistance settings. Often conducted in group classes with an instructor.

Sports massage

Deep tissue massage on muscles used in athletic exercise. Improves muscle balance and posture.

Steam room

A wooden treatment room which is heated to around 110°F. The steam opens the pores and eliminates toxins and aids respiration. Sugaring Ancient depilation treatment. A sticky sugary paste is applied to the skin and a strip of cloth or paper is pressed on top. The strip is removed quickly and takes with it unwanted hair.

Swedana

Hot herbal steam bath. Purifies and detoxifies through sweating. 1 of 2 preparatory treatments in purvakarma.

Swedish massage

Variety of massage techniques using oil. Improves circulation, reduces muscle tension.

Swiss shower

Powerful water jets on the body from various heights simulate an invigorating massage.

T'ai chi

Also known as: T'ai chi chuan.
A Chinese martial art form combining controlled breathing and visualisation with controlled stylised movements, to achieve balance, improved circulation and heightened mental clarity.

Tantra

Form of yoga involving strong, deep breathing and visualisation.

Temascal

Healing method attributed to indigenous North and Central American culture, involving gathering inside a domed structure where water is poured onto heated stones to produce steam. Detoxifies the skin.

Tepidarium

An open space that is heated. Used in ancient Rome as a room in which to prepare for a bath. Today, tepidaria often feature furniture on which to relax before and after treatments.

Thai herbal heat massage

Compress containing a combination of Thai healing herbs is heated and applied to the body to soothe aching muscles. Therapy may also incorporate acupressure and Thai stretches.
See also: Compress.

Thai massage

Traditionally performed on the floor, this dry massage originates from Thailand but is influenced by Chinese and Indian healing methods. Combines gentle rocking and slow stretches. Loose clothing is worn.

Shirodhara *Shangri-La's Villingili Resort and Spa, Maldives, Page 18*

Thai yoga massage

Combines massage techniques and acupressure with gentle yoga stretches. Therapists often also use their feet and elbows, focusing on the meridians to enhance energy flow.

Thalassotherapy

True thalassotherapy centres directly pump fresh seawater and use this for various therapies.

Thalasso cranial massage

Head, shoulder and neck massage performed in a warm pool.

Thermal bath

Warm body of water that is believed to have healing or beneficial properties.

Thermal sequencing

The combination of thermal treatment spaces, both hot and cold. The raising and lowering the body temperature stimulates circulation.

Thermal stamp therapy

Thermal massage complemented by the use of a thermal stamp. The stamp is a small bag filled with aromatic herbs, which is steamed before manipulating oils into the skin. Relaxes, soothes tight muscles and relieves inflamed skin.

Threading

Ancient method of hair removal from the Middle East and Asia. Cotton thread is wrapped around the hair and gently pulled to extract the hair from the root.

Tibetan bowls therapy

Also known as: Tibetan singing bowls. Treatment performed with the client fully clothed. A number of copper bowls are struck to produce waves of sound which resonate throughout the room. Believed to realign the body's natural rhythms and reduce stress.

Tisane

Also known as: Herbal tea.
Tisanes do not contain real tea leaves and are caffeine-free. They provide natural stimulation.

Tsubo shiatsu

A derivative of shiatsu developed by Hiroshi Ishizuka. Differs from shiatsu in that the practitioner uses their thumbs and palms on the tsubo or acupuncture points.
See also: Shiatsu; Meridian shiatsu; Zen shiatsu.

Tui na

Also known as: Tuina massage; Chinese tuina massage.
"Tui" means push in Chinese, while "na" means grasp. An important part of Traditional Chinese Medicine, tui na is a preventative technique used to treat specific internal ailments, using a wide variety of hand strokes. Stimulates the flow of qi, corrects imbalances. Therapist may use their fingers, hands, elbows and knees during the treatment.

Turkish bath

See: Hammam.

Ultrasound

Low frequency sound waves are used to effect subcutaneous rejuvenation. Employed in many different therapies, particularly for the face and for cellulite reduction.

Vamana

Potions are ingested to induce vomiting. This treatment is used to treat throat, chest and heart ailments as well as bronchitis. One of the purification techniques of purvakarma.

Vasti

Enemas used particularly for digestive imbalances. One of the purification techniques of purvakarma.

Vichy shower

Inspired by treatments in the French thermal spa city Vichy. The client is sprayed with water from micro-jets above the treatment bed. Improves circulation. May also include a massage.

Vietnamese massage

An invigorating massage using a combination of deep strokes. Stimulates blood and lymph circulation and improves skin tone and texture.

Vinotherapy

Therapeutic skin treatment using grapes and wine.

Virechana

A herbal tea is drunk with the intention of flushing out elements that may have clogged the digestive tracts. This is one of the 5 purification techniques of panchakarma.

Visualisation

This is a process of creating mental images to focus the mind for a more profound meditative experience.

Warm mist grotto

A warmed space filled with fine mist, sometimes enriched with herbal essences. The mist refreshes the skin and stimulates the airways.

Water walking

Low impact walking exercises with the lower half of the body in water. The water supports the body's weight and limits stress on the joints. Usually combined with conditioning exercises for the upper body.

Watsu

A healing massage therapy performed in a warm pool. The therapist guides the client's body in rhythmic movements, whilst also administering a pressure point massage.

Whitening facial

Treatment that brightens the skin, evens the skin tone and restores radiance.

Yoga

Ancient philosophy and practice involving mind and body and aimed at self-realisation. Various postures, "asanas", are adopted, with meditation and controlled breathing. The body is stretched and toned, circulation is improved.

Zen

The first documented account of Zen as a school of Buddhism in China dates to the 7th century CE. Central to Zen is the significance of experiential wisdom, particularly through meditation, in the pursuit of enlightenment.

Zen shiatsu

Also known as: Masunaga therapy.
A form of meridian shiatsu developed by Shizuto Masunaga. Differs from earlier forms of shiatsu in that the practitioner uses not only their thumbs and palms but also fists, elbows, and knees. Masunaga also developed a 2 hand style, in which 1 hand moves and applies pressure, while the other hand is stationary and provides support.
See also: Shiatsu; Meridian shiatsu; Tsubo shiatsu.

Zero balancing

Developed by Fritz Smith, MD. Gentle pressing is combined with stretching and bending to re-align the body structure and body energy and enhance physical, mental and spiritual well-being. The client remains clothed.

Symbols

The symbols on each spa page enable you to easily select a spa by its type and facilities.

☼ Day spa – guests can only visit for the duration of their treatments and no residential options are provided. Day Spas are open to non-residents when part of a hotel or resort or can be stand-alone.

🏷 Destination spa – the entire environment is geared towards wellness, health and relaxation. Accommodation is provided for spa clients only. Guests are often required to pre-book and enrol into a fixed, minimum period programme.

⇄ Hotel spa – part of a hotel or resort and generally only accessible to hotel guests, although in some cases day membership to non-residents is offered.

⊕ Medical spa – a spa offering medical services supervised or administered by medical professionals. A Medical Spa may specialise in diagnostic testing, preventive care, cosmetic procedures or a combination.

☁ Steam room

🌡 Sauna

⌂ Hammam

✳ Yoga / t'ai chi

≋ Indoor swimming pool

≋ Outdoor swimming pool

◎ Jacuzzi

H₂O Hydrotherapy / thalassotherapy

☾ Rasul room / pool

✳ Ice room

🚿 Multi-experience shower

🧴 Spa boutique

🍒 Spa cuisine

🏋 Gym

⚑ Golf

🏓 Tennis

♿ Wheelchair access to the public rooms and at least 1 bedroom

▮⁶ Number of single spa treatment rooms

▮▮⁶ Number of double / couple's spa treatment rooms

LIQUID ASSETS

www.hildon.com or ☎ +44 (0) 1794 302747

Luxury Spas Publishing Editor: Charlotte Drew

Production Manager: Kevin Bradbrook
Production Editor: Laura Kerry
Senior Designer: Rory Little
Copywriter: Francesca White

Publishing Director, Europe & The Mediterranean: Charlotte Evans
PA to Publishing Director: Nicola Sugden
Publishing Director, The Americas: Lesley O'Malley-Keyes
PA to Publishing Director: Jennifer Power
Marketing Manager: Adam Crabtree
Digital Marketing Manager: Gemma James
Client Services Director: Fiona Patrick
Managing Director: Andrew Warren
PA to Managing Director: Amelia Priday

CONDÉ NAST
JOHANSENS

Front Cover Image: Shangri-La Hotel, Qaryat Al Beri, Abu Dhabi, United Arab Emirates, Page 35
Back Cover Image: Hilton Maldives Iru Fushi Resort & Spa, Page 17
This Page: Shangri-La's Rasa Sayang Resort & Spa, Malaysia, Page 55